MARINADES
MAKE ORDINARY FOODS EXTRAORDINARY

Dona Z. Meilach

BRISTOL PUBLISHING ENTERPRISES, INC.
San Leandro, California

A NITTY GRITTY® COOKBOOK

Printed in the United States of America.

ISBN 1-55867-119-6

Front cover design: Frank Paredes
Front cover photography: John Benson
Food stylist: Suzanne Carreiro
Back cover photography: Bushnell/Golfer

CONTENTS

THE MAGIC OF MARINADES

A marinade can make ordinary cooking extraordinary. A marinade can enhance the flavor of good foods and add interesting tastes to bland foods. It can make tough foods tender and impart savory tangs to leftovers.

WHAT IS A MARINADE?

It's an easy-to-mix seasoned liquid in which foods are soaked.

With their simple combination of ingredients, marinades have nearly magical powers. They break down and tenderize tough fibrous elements in meats, poultry and game. In addition to adding flavors, they preserve many foods. They introduce variety to everyday menus. And they help save you money.

What kinds of foods can be marinated? Raw meats, fish, poultry, game, vegetables and fruits can be subjected to the wizardry of marinades. The results will be spectacular appetizers, salads, entrées and desserts.

Marinated foods can be added to and combined with other foods. Flavored vegetables will perk up soups. Marinated (often called macerated) fruits are palate-pleasers when added to puddings, pies and cakes.

Some marinated foods are eaten raw and some are cooked. If cooked, they may be prepared by every method normally used: roasting, broiling, microwaving, frying and grilling.

FOREIGN FLAVORS

For centuries, countless cultures have used marinades in their traditional recipes for essentially the same reasons that we use them today. In fact, fabulously flavored foods from many foreign countries have inspired an increased awareness and use of marinades. Magazines and newspapers feature menus from China, Japan, Burma, India, North Africa, Denmark, Sweden and other countries. Food writers and their readers try the recipes, experiment, and often adapt them to American tastes and available ingredients.

ECONOMY

In addition to the new tastes and pungent aromas offered by marinated foods, there's another important benefit: marinades can help offset food costs. By using marinades, less costly cuts of beef, pork, lamb and veal can be flavored and tenderized so they rival the taste and texture of choice cuts. Abundant supplies of in-season foods can be preserved with a marinade and used out of season. Foods that lose some of their inherent flavoring, fragrance and texture through freezing or other storage methods can be salvaged with a marinade.

The costs of using a marinade are minimal as is the effort involved. The last-minute cook may have to alter procedures slightly because marinades must be prepared ahead and foods are soaked in them from one hour to three days before preparing or serving (unless you own a speed-marinating device, which we will discuss in a later section on equipment). However, cooking time is often reduced, sometimes by as much as one-third.

TAKING THE MYSTERY OUT OF THE MAGIC

Once you know the secrets, you, too, can effortlessly pull the rabbit out of the hat. Marinating is an easy trick to learn. In the simplest terms, a marinade consists of just a few basic ingredients:

- an acid, such as vinegar, wine, lemon juice or beer. Acids break down fibers, tenderizing them and allowing the flavors to enter. Acids also help retard bacterial growth and help preserve the foods soaked in them.
- seasonings such as herbs or spices. Seasonings add delicious flavors. Salt and sugar or honey have several functions: they impart flavor, heighten the flavors of other ingredients, preserve food and help retard bacterial growth.
- sometimes an oil, such as olive oil or vegetable oil. Oil adds moisture and smoothness, and in the case of olive oil, it also adds some flavor. Oil helps to carry flavorings into the fibers.

Ideally, a marinade should whisper and subtly enhance the food, not overpower it. If all foods marinated in a soy sauce base tasted like soy sauce, rather than the foods themselves, the whole point of marinating would be missed.

The recipes offered are designed so that you may cook "by the book." But if you like to revamp and invent tasty recipes, do so. You can select a basic marinade and, by changing the herbs and spices and the liquid base, completely alter the character of the food.

MARINADE BASICS

Before you begin, you should bear in mind a few tricks of the trade so that every performance will be successful.

- It is preferable to marinate foods in a glass, ceramic, enamel or stainless steel container, because acids react to cast iron, aluminum or copper, causing chemical changes, rust and bitter tastes. Marinating in plastic is not recommended when using the same plastic container repeatedly, because over time plastic can absorb oils and flavors that cannot easily be washed away. However, there are exceptions. New marinating equipment made of plastic works so quickly that this problem is solved. Disposable plastics make marinating convenient and safe: you can put the marinade in a locking food storage bag with the food and place the bag in a low bowl, turning the bag occasionally so that all the pieces of food are covered with the marinade. When the food has been marinated, the bag is discarded.

- Always blend the marinade ingredients well. Stir them with a wooden spoon, shake them in a jar, or mix them in a blender or food processor.

- Foods to be marinated less than 1 hour may be left out at room temperature. For longer marinating times, store foods in the refrigerator in a covered dish or sealed bag so that strong seasonings won't reach other foods. *Foods that are marinated for long periods at room temperature can be subject to dangerous bacterial growth.*

- Always marinate fresh or completely thawed foods. Do not marinate frozen foods, as the thawed liquid will dilute the marinade. Wipe and dry foods with a paper towel before immersing them in the marinade.

- Foods that have already been marinated may be frozen before they are cooked, if they have not been previously frozen. For example, if you wish to marinate enough meat to make kabobs for three meals, triple the recipe. Use only the meat you need for one meal, skewer the remaining meat, wrap individual servings and freeze. Freeze some of the marinade in a container and use it to brush the food during cooking. You can thaw the meat while you prepare the rest of the meal.

- The amount of marinade needed varies with the type of food. Some recipes call for completely immersing the food in the marinade. Others, such as recipes for beef, require less marinade liquid, but the food must be turned occasionally in the marinade so all portions are eventually immersed.

- Marinating time varies by food. The tougher the meat, for example, the longer the marinating period --- perhaps as long as two days. Delicate fish may require only an hour to marinate.

- The marinade liquid may be prepared in advance and stored in a jar in the refrigerator overnight or until ready to use. This allows time for flavors to develop. Fresh herbs and spices require more time than dried ones. Use fresh ingredients for overnight marinades and dried and ground herbs and spices for shorter periods.

- Usually, although not always, the marinade is drained from the dish before the food is cooked. The marinade may be reserved for basting or for thickening juices used for sauces and gravies. ***Reserved marinades must be boiled for at least three minutes after meats, fish and poultry are removed from them, as they may be subject to dangerous bacterial growth****. **Marinades should not be kept and reused.***

- Marinated foods may be cooked by any recipe given or by methods you already know well for a particular food. Marinades given for kabobs can be used in a baked dish. A recipe that calls for baking may be adapted for the grill, the microwave or the skillet. Generally, because the foods are tenderized, cooking time may be reduced by as much as one-third. Use a meat thermometer for meats, poultry and fish.

EQUIPMENT

Very little is needed in the way of special equipment. You will need containers to hold the food and the liquid, preferably of glass, ceramic, stainless steel or enamelware. You may wish to use locking food storage bags. You will need other standard kitchen equipment such as measuring cups and spoons, shaker jars, knives, a cutting board and perhaps a garlic press. A blender or food processor is a useful convenience.

New devices have recently been introduced that marinate quickly by creating a vacuum and drawing the marinating liquid into the food in just minutes.

- The **Minute Marinizer**, by Toastmaster, is an electric appliance that creates a vacuum in an airtight container which holds the food and the marinade, drawing the marinade into the food instantly. This unit operates with the push of a button, and the bowl and cover are dishwasher-safe. Call 800-947-3744 to find a source near you.

- ISI North America offers the **MicroMarinader**, a covered dish with a manually operated pump handle that fits into an opening in the lid. After a vacuum is created, the marinade permeates the food in seconds. Call 800-447-2426 to find the location of a store near you that carries this item.

- The **Quick Flavor Vacuum Marinator** from Progressive International is also a unit with a manually operated pump connected to a covered container with a hose attachment. After you place your food in the container with the marinade, you pump the air out of the container and refrigerate it for 10 to 20 minutes. The number to call for more information is 800-426-7101.

- **Food$aver**, a home vacuum packaging system made by Tilia, Inc., also allows you to marinate quickly (15 to 20 minutes) by vacuum packing the food and marinade in a Food$aver Canister. Each Food$aver comes with a hose attachment and jar sealer to be used with jars or Canisters, which may be purchased in several sizes. With this marinade system, you have the added advantage of home food storage for shelf or freezer. Call 800-777-5452 for more information.

INGREDIENTS

Ingredients for marinades should be of good quality and fresh when available. Dried herbs and spices, seasoned salts, extracts and flavorings may be used, but remember that their shelf life is limited; they lose their strength after eight to twelve months. Vegetable oils have only a three- or four-month shelf life.

Acids include vinegar, wine, brandy, vermouth, beer and other alcohol-based liquids, as well as lemon, lime, orange, grapefruit and tomato juices. Two or more acids may be combined in a recipe to alter the flavor, such as vinegar and orange juice.

Marinades can be flavored by spices and herbs such as basil, coriander, thyme, rosemary, tarragon, parsley, cumin and any of your personal favorites. They can also be flavored with salt, sugar and honey.

Olive oil or any of the variety of vegetable oils may be used. When oil is used, the ratio of oil to acid varies with the type of food.

Salt and sugar are not always used. Salt may be omitted from some beef recipes because it tends to draw out natural juices. Many acids, such as beer, soy sauce, tomato juice and catsup, already contain sugar and salt. Some people wish to reduce the amounts of salt, fat and sugar in their diets and omit all three of these ingredients.

Prepared salad dressings, such as French, Italian and Caesar dressing (including low calorie and low fat versions) can be used alone as a marinade or with additional amounts of any flavorings. There are prepared marinade additives containing mixtures of spices such as lemon and peppercorn. There are prepackaged meat, fish and poultry marinades that have to be mixed with water or wine. These flavor foods in only about fifteen minutes, but some are quite strong and very salty, so use them carefully.

You can premix your favorite combinations of herbs and spices and have them handy for easy use. Instead of buying expensive flavored vinegars, you can make you own (see page 13).

Most marinade recipes are mixed as liquids at room temperature. Those that are cooked should be cooled to room temperature or chilled before adding them to the food. A dry marinade is a mixture of herbs and spices; when rubbed on foods with natural juices, the juices mix with the dry ingredients, creating a liquid marinade.

Possible substitutes for ingredients are listed at the end of this chapter.

INGREDIENTS REFERENCE LIST

anise: a plant that yields seeds, roots and leaves. Usually the seeds are available commercially; they have a licorice-like flavor.

beer: an acid. Any kind can be used. "Light" and alcohol-free beer have fewer calories than regular beer.

chives: an herb of the onion family with a delicate, mild onion flavor. Use chives fresh from the grocery store or grow them in pots on a windowsill or in an herb garden. The more chives are cut, the faster they grow. The blue flowers, as well as the leaves, may be used in salads.

coconut milk: frequently used in recipes for marinades and sauces from Southeast Asia. Milk can be taken from a fresh coconut or purchased in cans. If a fresh coconut is used, the coconut meat should be cut into chunks and soaked in water to cover. Squeeze out or mash the coconut in a food processor and strain out the milk. Freshly grated coconut can be used to garnish foods.

cumin: a seed with a hot, bitter, piquant flavor used to season Middle Eastern stews and chili.

curry powder: a blend of up to 20 spices and herbs, including cumin, coriander, cayenne and turmeric.

dill seed: the fruit of dill weed, the seed has a sharp and pungent taste and is often used in Scandinavian recipes and in Middle Eastern dishes, sometimes accompanied by mint. Dill *weed* has a milder flavor.

fruit juice and grated rind: orange, grapefruit, lemon, lime and tomato juices can be used. The juices add essential acid and preservative ingredients. Grated rinds add aroma and flavor. Citrus juices prevent bananas, pears, peaches and other fruits from turning brown.

garlic: a small bulb that breaks into individual cloves. Always use fresh garlic, if possible, rather than garlic salt or powder, which can become stale and impart an "off" flavor to a marinade. Garlic may be minced or slivered, or its juice can be obtained by squeezing a clove through a garlic press.

hoisin sauce: used in Oriental cooking and marinades as a seasoning. It is a dark, rich sauce made from soybeans.

honey: available with clover, orange or other flavors. (Also see sugar.)

hot pepper sauce: ready-made or homemade. You may buy commercial hot pepper sauces such as Tabasco Sauce or make your own by stirring together 1 tbs. cayenne pepper, 2 tbs. sesame or vegetable oil and 1/2 tsp. sesame seeds. When used in marinades, do not store marinade longer than 48 hours.

juniper berries: a purple-black fruit of an evergreen bush, available dried. The berries may be used whole or lightly crushed. They impart a sweet, rich taste.

liqueurs: commercial or homemade. Fruit flavors are popular for marinades.

liquor: a distilled alcoholic beverage made from grains or other plants, such as whiskey, gin, vodka or gum. All alcohol-basic liquids are acids.

mint: fresh or dried mint leaves are often added to lamb and pork marinades.

mixed herbs: sold commercially, usually as a blend of rosemary, basil, thyme and marjoram. Other combinations are available.

mustard: made from mustard seeds and used as a flavoring in many of the marinades. Mustard is used in two forms: Prepared mustard is available in different types, strengths and flavors. Most of the interesting mustards are Dijon-style and come from France. Some contain spices that may be noted on the label, such as tarragon, dill, thyme or peppercorn, and some are mixed with wines. German mustards are sweeter and have less bite than French mustards. Dry mustard powder (ground yellow mustard seed) is available on the grocer's spice shelf.

oils: olive oil and vegetable oil are both used in marinade recipes. Oils vary in quality, taste, price and amount of saturated fat. Olive oil is available in different grades, depending on which pressing of the olive was used. The finest and highest-priced olive oil is taken from the first pressing of the olives and labeled virgin olive oil. The lowest quality is made from the fruit and cracked pits. Vegetable oils are made from corn, cottonseed, rapeseed (canola oil), safflower and sunflower seed, soybeans or peanuts. Generally, any oil can be used interchangeably in the recipes that call for vegetable oil. Olive oil and vegetable oil may be mixed half and half for economy. Some newcomers are walnut oil and artichoke oil, which impart special flavors. Oils should not be refrigerated, as they turn cloudy, but if left on the shelf and not tightly capped, they can become rancid in time. Buy quantities proportional to your use of them over a reasonable period of time. Shelf life is three to four months.

onions: for recipes that call for onions, any variety will do — white, yellow or pearl onions. Red and Italian onions are sweeter and more decorative than white and yellow onions. Green onions, also called scallions, are fresh young onions with a small white bulb and leafy green top. The bulb and all but about an inch of the very top of the leafy portion may be used for flavoring. Chives, scallions and shallots are from the onion family, have different tastes and may be substituted for each other.

onion juice: to make, grate a large onion on a grater or chop in a blender or food processer. Strain.

paprika: not simply a colorful garnish, paprika flavors range from mild to pungent andhot.

parsley: used for flavoring and garnish. Fresh parsley is preferred as it is available year-round.

peppercorns: peppercorns are ground to make familiar black, red and white peppers. Green peppercorns are packed in water and may be used with marinades and added to prepared mustard for a zippier flavor. Buy pepper already ground, or grind it yourself. Some recipes call for unground peppercorns.

peppers: there are many varieties. Red pepper is the universal name for chili peppers. Crushed red pepper (dried red pepper flakes) is very hot, and cayenne powdered red pepper is even hotter. Both of these easily available varieties should be used judiciously. Red chili peppers are also available fresh or dried whole. Green chili peppers, fresh or packed in liquid in cans, may be substituted for hot red peppers, and range from mild to very hot. Jalapeño green chili peppers are popular because they are readily available and can be easily seeded (seeds and veins are much hotter than the peppers themselves).

salt: a basic component in many meat, fish and vegetable recipes, is a mineral (not a spice or an herb). It adds flavor and enhances other ingredients. When used with sugar or sweet foods, it sharpens the sweetness. Ordinary table salt, which is fine and quite intense in flavor, should be used sparingly. When doubling a recipe, it is not necessary to double the amount of salt. Use a minimal amount of salt in meat recipes as it tends to draw out juices. It is more important in fish marinades, as drawing out moisture makes fish flesh firmer and tastier. Kosher salt, which has no additives, is coarse in texture and less salty than table salt. Sea salt, usually sold in health food stores, comes in fine and coarse varieties. People on salt-free diets can substitute lemon or lime juice for salt in equal amounts.

shallots: a member of the onion family, shallots are formed more like garlic than onions, with multiple cloves in each bulb. Shallots have a mild onion flavor.

soy sauce: a basic ingredient in many Oriental dishes and in all teriyaki recipes. Black soy sauce is dark, rich and full-bodied; light soy sauce has a more delicate taste than the dark. Reduced sodium soy sauces are also available.

stock (chicken or beef): Use homemade stock with fat removed, canned stock or broth made from bouillon cubes. Japanese miso may be substituted as a liquid stock.

sugar: white sugar, brown sugar or a mild-flavored honey may be used in marinades. Sugar, like salt and acids, draws out flavor and prevents bacterial growth.

tarragon: a fresh or dried licorice-flavored leafy herb that gives a special tang to marinades.

thyme: a garden variety herb that may be grown at home and used fresh. It is also available dried.

vermouth: fortified white wine, usually dry, that has been flavored with herbs and spices. Sweet vermouth is reddish brown (colored with caramel). A third vermouth is white and slightly sweet. Dry vermouth and dry white wine may be used interchangeably, and so may red wine and red vermouth.

vinegar: an acid component of marinades that helps preserve foods and break down fibers. Vinegars are the result of fermentation of an alcohol produced from the juice of fruits such as berries, apples and grapes. There are white and red vinegars, white wine and red wine vinegars, herb and spice vinegars and garlic vinegars. You can create your own flavored vinegars using two methods:

1. Heat 1 pt. plain vinegar or red or white wine vinegar to boiling. Pour over 1 tbs. dried herbs or spices of your choice in a 1-pint sterilized bottle. Cool and seal. If fresh herbs are available, use one sprig for each pint of vinegar.
2. Add herbs and/or spices in the same proportion as with the previous method to cold vinegar. Steep for 4 weeks. Filter the vinegar. Rebottle it in sterilized containers and keep it tightly corked.

Suggested combinations include vinegar with tarragon, dill, rosemary, basil, marjoram or oregano. A clove of minced garlic or a tablespoon of minced onion may be added, if desired. If garlic is used, crush the clove and remove it after 24 hours.

wine: dry or sweet red wines, such as Burgundy, port, rosé and sherry, or dry and sweet white wines, such as chablis and riesling, can be used. When wines sit on a shelf too long, they turn to vinegar and can be used as wine vinegar in recipes calling for that ingredient.

yogurt: milk fermented by certain bacteria growing under controlled time and temperature conditions. It is smooth, creamy, rich and slightly tart. Marinades composed of yogurts and used on meats tend to break down the meat fibers, thereby making them more easily digestible.

SUGGESTED SUBSTITUTES

garlic: use an equal amount of shallots or scallions

herbs: 1 tbs. fresh herbs equals $1/3$ tsp. dried

honey: 1 cup equals 1 cup packed brown sugar or 1 cup white sugar

juniper berries: use an equal amount of red jelly or jam

mustard, prepared: use an equal amount of dry mustard mixed with water, wine, vinegar, lemon juice or milk to the consistency of prepared mustard

oils: vegetable oils or olive oil or mixtures of half vegetable oil and half olive oil

onions: use an equal amount of chives or scallions or shallots

salt: use an equal amount of lemon or lime juice

shallots: use an equal amount of scallions

spices: approximately 1 tbs. fresh for $1/3$ tsp. dried or ground (example: ginger)

tarragon vinegar: white vinegar with a touch of crumbled tarragon leaves

vermouth, red: use an equal amount of red wine

vermouth, dry: use an equal amount of dry white wine, dry sherry or sake

vinegar: use an equal amount of any other acidic liquid

wine: use an equal amount of vermouth, or mix water with another acidic liquid such as vinegar or lemon juice in equal parts

yogurt: use an equal amount of sour cream, or low fat or nonfat sour cream

MARINATED APPETIZERS

Marinated appetizers look good, smell delicious, taste superb and convey a mysterious appeal that is hard to pinpoint. You have probably eaten many of the marvelous appetizers prepared by marinating — herring, rumaki, mushrooms, beef and chicken kabobs, fruits in wine, radishes in wine. The range of delicate differences in hot and cold, sweet and tart, salty and spicy tastes is vast when marinades are used.

This chapter includes several appetizers from foreign cuisines. Many utilize essentially the same ingredients with only a few characteristic differences. Dill, for instance, is found in Swedish recipes. Olive oil is used in most Italian appetizers. Peanut oil is used in Eastern recipes. Soy sauce is indigenous to anything called teriyaki. A Hawaiian marinade usually calls for pineapple juice.

Fruit appetizers are easy to make. Almost all fresh, frozen and drained canned fruits can be marinated in a compatible liqueur, brandy or wine for 1 to 2 hours before serving.

Always serve appetizers attractively with colorful garnishes for eye appeal as well as taste appeal.

MINTED MELON ON SKEWERS

MARINADE
¼ cup crème de menthe
¼ cup lime juice
¼ cup white wine
1 tsp. poppy seeds

1 cup cantaloupe balls or cubes
1 cup watermelon balls or triangles
1 cup honeydew balls or wedges

1 cup Persian or Crenshaw melon cubes
  or balls, or any combination of
  seasonal melon pieces
mint leaves for garnish, optional

Mix marinade ingredients and pour over melon pieces in a bowl. Refrigerate, covered, for 3 hours. Drain. Thread melon pieces on short wooden skewers and pierce skewer tips into half of a watermelon shell placed upside down on a platter. Add mint leaves or other garnish in season. Makes about 6 servings.

FRUIT WITH WINE MARINADE

MARINADE

½ cup dry red wine
¼ cup cherry juice
¼ cup grape or currant jelly
1 tbs. lemon or lime juice
⅛ tsp. salt

---

1 cup pitted canned red cherries, drained, juice reserved
1 cup diced fresh or canned orange sections or mandarin oranges

1 cup fresh pineapple or pear chunks, grapes, or other fruit in season, diced into bite-sized pieces, or use frozen

Heat wine and cherry juice to simmering; add jelly and stir until melted. Remove from heat and add lemon or lime juice and salt. Cool. Drain fruits and combine in a bowl. Pour marinade over fruits and cover. Chill several hours. Serve heaped in cocktail glasses with some marinade poured over fruit. Makes 6 servings.

PLUM AND BACON APPETIZERS

MARINADE
1 cup soy sauce
1/4 cup brown sugar, firmly packed
3 tbs. wine vinegar
3 tbs. dry sherry
2 cloves garlic, minced

12 fresh Italian prune plums
3 oz. sharp cheddar cheese, cut into twelve 1/4-inch cubes
12 slices bacon

Slit one side of each plum only enough to remove pit and leave plum whole. Mix marinade ingredients in a medium saucepan. Add plums and heat to boiling. Reduce heat and simmer for 2 minutes. Marinate in the refrigerator, covered, for 4 hours.

Just before serving, drain plums. Place 1 cheese cube in each plum, wrap 1 bacon strip around each plum and secure with a presoaked wooden pick. Place plums on a wire rack over a baking pan to catch bacon fat. Broil 4 inches from heat, turning once, until bacon is crisp, about 4 minutes each side. Makes 12.

ROSY RADISHES

MARINADE

½ cup vegetable oil
⅔ cup wine vinegar
¼ cup cold water
½ tsp. pepper
¾ tsp. salt
⅛ tsp. dried onion flakes

2 bunches large radishes, washed and trimmed
½ tsp. salt
water

Put radishes in a small saucepan with ½ tsp. salt and enough water to cover. Bring to a boil and boil for 2 minutes. Drain. Mix marinade ingredients and place in a jar with radishes. Cover tightly and marinate for 2 days in the refrigerator. This dish will keep in the refrigerator for about 1 week. Serve in a bowl or on a platter. Makes 2 to 3 dozen.

MARINATED MUSHROOMS

MARINADE

½ cup water
3 tbs. lemon juice
1 tsp. salt
1 clove garlic, minced
1 bay leaf
1 small onion, sliced

½ cup olive oil
1 tbs. green peppercorns
1 tsp. fresh tarragon, or ⅓ tsp. dried
1 tsp. celery seed
¼ tsp. whole cloves

1½-2 lb. fresh button mushrooms, stems removed

Combine water, lemon juice, salt, garlic and bay leaf. Bring to a boil in a medium saucepan. Reduce heat and simmer, uncovered, for 5 minutes. Add mushrooms and onion and simmer for 1 minute. Transfer to a medium bowl or covered jar. Stir in remaining ingredients and refrigerate overnight or for 1 to 2 days. Drain and serve on an appetizer platter or on unbuttered thin rounds of French bread. Makes 24 to 36 mushrooms.

MARINATED JICAMA

MARINADE

3 tbs. orange juice
3 tbs. grapefruit juice
2 tbs. lemon or lime juice
1 tsp. finely grated grapefruit or
orange rind
1 tbs. finely chopped fresh coriander,
or 2 tsp. ground

1½ lb. jicama (1 large or 2 small)
1 large sweet orange, cut into wedges

Peel jicama with a sharp knife or potato peeler and cut it into ½-inch cubes. Mix marinade, pour over jicama and refrigerate, covered, for at least 1 hour. Arrange on a platter and garnish with orange wedges. Makes 8 to 10 servings.

NOTE: Jicama (say HICK-AMA) is a bulbous root that looks like a turnip and is indigenous to Mexico, sometimes called *Mexican potato*. It is becoming more and more popular in the United States. The root is peeled to reveal a white crunchy flesh that is sweet and slightly nutty in flavor. It is good both raw and cooked. Left as is, it makes a perfect addition to a raw vegetable platter presented with a dipping sauce. This recipe gives it a special flavor.

MARINATED COCKTAIL BEETS

MARINADE

2 cups tarragon vinegar
4 heaping tbs. brown sugar
2 large onions, minced
2 cloves garlic, mashed
2 tsp. dry mustard
2 tsp. salt
1 tsp. pepper

2 cans (1 lb. each) whole baby beets, drained

Mix marinade and pour over beets. Cover and marinate in the refrigerator at least overnight. Drain and serve. Makes about 48 beets.

MARINATED CARROT SLICES OR STICKS

MARINADE

1/4 cup olive oil
2 tbs. wine vinegar
2 cloves garlic, minced
1 tsp. dried oregano
1/2 tsp. salt
1/2 tsp. pepper

8-10 large carrots
1/4 cup water

Peel carrots and cut into 1/2-inch slices or 1/2-inch-long matchsticks. Steam or microwave with 1/4 cup water until crisp-tender. Drain. Place in a bowl with marinade ingredients and mix well. Marinate covered for at least 12 hours. Drain and serve on an appetizer platter. Makes 8 to 10 servings.

RUMAKI

MARINADE I

½ cup dry red wine, or dry sherry
⅓ cup soy sauce
1 cup canned beef stock
3 tbs. lemon or lime juice
2 tbs. brown sugar, or honey
1 clove garlic, mashed
¼ cup chopped green onion
½ tsp. salt

MARINADE II

1 cup soy sauce
6 tbs. orange-flavored liqueur
2 cloves garlic, chopped

1 lb. chicken livers
1 small can water chestnuts, drained

1 lb. bacon slices, cut in half crosswise

Cut chicken livers in half. Cut water chestnuts into thirds. Combine ingredients for the marinade of your choice. Marinate livers and water chestnuts in the refrigerator for 4 hours. Drain. Wrap a piece of chicken liver and a piece of water chestnut together with each bacon slice. Secure with a toothpick. Broil on a rack over a baking pan to catch bacon grease, 3 to 4 inches from heat, for about 10 minutes, or until bacon is crisp. Turn occasionally. Rumaki may also be cooked on a grill. Makes about 16 servings.

INDONESIAN SATÉS

MARINADE
4 tbs. chili seasoning mix*
1/4 cup water
1/3 cup vegetable oil
4 tbs. lemon juice

2½ lb. chicken breasts, skinned, boned and cut into 1- to 1½-inch cubes

Combine 4 tbs. chili seasoning mix with water, oil and lemon juice. Mix well and pour over chicken. Stir gently, cover and marinate in the refrigerator for 4 hours. Remove chicken from marinade and arrange on small wooden skewers that have been soaked in water. Broil or grill for 4 minutes on each side, brushing with marinade. Serve with *Peanut Sauce*, page 27. Makes 8 to 10 servings.

*Purchase 1 envelope (1½ oz.) chili seasoning mix and divide it for use in marinade and sauce.

NOTE: Satés are dainty, skewered, grilled meats often sold at public gatherings in Indonesia, similar to the sale of hot dogs at American functions. This recipe uses chicken, but pork, lamb, beef or veal may be substituted. Prepare marinated skewered satés in advance and let guests cook their own over an indoor or outdoor grill.

PEANUT SAUCE

remaining chili seasoning mix (about 1 tsp.)*
¾ cup water
1 tbs. lemon juice
¼ cup chunky peanut butter
1 tbs. chopped green onion for garnish

In a small saucepan, combine chili seasoning mix, water, lemon juice and peanut butter. Bring to a boil, stirring constantly, and cook until thickened. Garnish with green onion.

* See page 26.

BROILED SESAME CHICKEN

MARINADE
½ cup soy sauce
½ cup white wine, or sake
½ cup sesame oil
1 large clove garlic, crushed
1 tbs. grated or minced ginger root
1½ tsp. sugar

1-1½ lb. chicken, boned and cut into bite-sized pieces
½ cup toasted sesame seeds*

Mix marinade and pour over chicken pieces in a flat dish. Marinate for 1 hour or more, turning chicken once or twice. Drain and place pieces on wooden skewers that have been soaked in water. Broil for 5 to 6 minutes, turning once. Roll in sesame seeds and serve hot. Makes 4 to 6 servings.

*Toast sesame seeds in a 350° oven for 20 minutes, stirring frequently to prevent burning.

ORIENTAL CHICKEN WINGS

MARINADE

½ cup soy sauce
¼ cup Madeira wine, or sherry
¼ cup pineapple juice
¼ cup orange juice

¼ cup dark brown sugar, firmly
  packed
1 tsp. finely minced ginger root
1 tsp. lemon juice

3 lb. chicken wings
¾ cup flour

¼ cup freshly grated Parmesan cheese
1½ cups vegetable oil for deep frying

Remove and discard chicken wing tips; cut wings in half at the joint. Combine marinade ingredients in a bowl. Add chicken pieces and stir to coat well. Refrigerate, covered, stirring once, for 6 hours or overnight. On a piece of waxed paper, combine flour and Parmesan cheese. Drain chicken. Roll chicken pieces in flour-cheese mixture to coat. Heat oil in a skillet to 365° and fry wings a few at a time until golden and cooked through, about 3 minutes. Drain on paper towels and keep warm while frying remaining wings. Or, bake in a preheated 325° oven for about 45 minutes, and then broil quickly on both sides until crisp. Makes 18 servings.

NOTE: This recipe may be prepared ahead of time and warmed in the oven or microwaved before serving.

PEACH-FLAVORED GLAZED HAM CUBES

MARINADE

1 tbs. soy sauce
3 tbs. peach-flavored brandy or
liqueur
2 tsp. lemon juice

---

1 cup cooked ham, cut into ¾-inch cubes

Mix marinade ingredients and stir into ham cubes until they are completely covered. Marinate for 1 hour. Drain and heat under the broiler for about 3 to 4 minutes, turning with a spoon so all sides are glazed. Makes 4 to 6 servings.

BRANDIED BEEF KABOBS

MARINADE
½ cup brandy
¼ cup vegetable oil
½ tsp. salt

¾ lb. beef top round, cut into thin strips

Mix marinade and pour over beef. Marinate for several hours or overnight in the refrigerator. Thread beef onto short wooden skewers that have been soaked in water and broil quickly, turning only once, or let guests cook their own over a grill. Makes about 24 appetizers.

SEVICHE

MARINADE

1/4 cup olive oil
1 1/2-2 cups fresh lime or lemon juice
1 tomato, skinned, seeded and
  chopped

1/4 cup diced red onion
1 can (4 oz.) diced green chiles
1/3 tsp. mashed garlic
pepper to taste

1 lb. very fresh fillets of mackerel, cod, sole, bass or grouper
OR
1 lb. shrimp and scallops
parsley sprigs, avocado slices, or lemon or lime slices for garnish

Combine marinade with fish and mix well. Refrigerate, covered, stirring occasionally, until fish becomes opaque, for at least 8 hours or overnight. Garnish with parsley sprigs, avocado slices, or lemon or lime slices. Serve cold. Makes 6 to 8 servings.

NOTE: This is the Latin American version of raw fish. *Seviche* comes from the verb *cebar*, meaning "to saturate." Marinated raw fish is found in many cultures.

LOMILOMI SALMON IN CHERRY TOMATOES

MARINADE
1 cup lime juice
1 large onion, minced
1½ tsp. white pepper
¼ tsp. sugar
¼ tsp. hot pepper sauce

1½ lb. salted salmon, cut into ¼-inch cubes
3 pt. large cherry tomatoes, hollowed out
green onions or parsley for garnish

Place salmon cubes in marinade mixture. Refrigerate, covered, stirring occasionally, for 6 hours or overnight. Stuff salmon mixture into hollowed-out cherry tomatoes for individual appetizer servings. Garnish with green onions or parsley. Makes 12 to 14 servings.

NOTE: This is the Hawaiian version of marinated raw salmon.

MARINATED HERRING

MARINADE
1 cup vinegar
1 tbs. pickling spices
3 tbs. sugar

2-3 herring, cleaned and filleted into 2-inch pieces
1 onion, sliced
sour cream

Place herring pieces in a 2-quart glass jar or crock, alternating with onion slices. Mix marinade and pour over herring. Store in the refrigerator, covered, for 5 to 7 days. Serve with sour cream. Makes 6 servings.

MEXICAN MARINATED FRIED FISH

MARINADE
1½ cups olive oil
½ cup white wine vinegar
⅓ cup dry white wine, or vodka
capers, salt and freshly ground
pepper to taste

1½ lb. flounder or other white fish
   fillets, cut into 1½-x-½-inch pieces
1 cup flour
1 tsp. salt

¼ tsp. white pepper
¼ cup vegetable oil
¼ cup unsalted butter
2 medium-sized red onions, thinly sliced

Combine flour, salt and white pepper and coat fish with flour mixture. Heat oil and butter in a skillet over medium high heat. Sauté fish, turning frequently, for 3 to 5 minutes or until golden. Place a layer of sautéed fish in a 1½-quart baking dish and layer with sliced onions. Mix marinade and pour over onions and fish. Place capers, salt and pepper on top. Refrigerate, covered, spooning marinade liquid over fish several times. Marinate 4 hours or overnight. Let stand at room temperature for 20 minutes before serving. Makes 6 servings.

RUMAKI-STYLE ZESTY SHRIMP

MARINADE
½ cup chili sauce
½ clove garlic, minced

1 cup cleaned, cooked shrimp (fresh or frozen)
8-10 bacon slices, cut in half crosswise

Combine shrimp in marinade mixture. Cover and refrigerate for 4 hours, stirring occasionally. Fry bacon slices until nearly cooked but not crisp. Drain. Wrap each shrimp in a bacon slice and secure with a wooden pick. Broil 2 to 3 inches from heat until bacon is crisp. Makes 18.

SHRIMP IN MARINADE

MARINADE
1¼ cups vegetable oil
½ cup white wine vinegar
2 tsp. celery seed
1 tsp. salt
dash hot pepper sauce

2 lb. cooked, peeled, deveined shrimp
1 cup chopped green onions

Alternate layers of shrimp and green onions in a flat glass dish. Mix marinade and pour over shrimp. Cover and store in the refrigerator for 12 hours. Stir gently. Serve in a cocktail dish on shredded lettuce or directly from dish with cocktail picks. Makes 4 to 6 servings.

MARINATED VEGETABLES

Marinated vegetables are delicious and pretty. And they keep so well, they are still good the second day. Traditional three-bean salads, mixed vegetables and button mushrooms make dynamic luncheon additions and dinner accompaniments.

Flavor, appearance and convenience are only a part of the bounty you get when you soak vegetables in wines and vinegars rather than splashing them with a dressing. The many variations on niçoise salads are the results of marinating vegetables in French-style dressing. Pickling, a first cousin to marinating, enables us to buy large quantities of in-season vegetables and preserve them for out-of-season treats.

Marinade ingredients should be mixed thoroughly before adding them to the vegetables. Then refrigerate all together in a marinade-safe container for at least an hour. Fibrous vegetables such as beans, peas, tomatoes, carrots, cucumbers, zucchini, artichokes, mushrooms, asparagus and broccoli are best for marinating. Vegetables may be marinated raw or cooked.

Try the combinations suggested in this chapter, and then use your imagination to make medleys and mixtures of your own. Switch and substitute your favorite ingredients both in the vegetables and in the marinades.

Drain and reserve marinated vegetable juices before serving. Then freeze or refrigerate the juices and use them in soups. The juices contain abundant minerals and vitamins and the flavor is mild because the vegetables have absorbed most of the vinegar.

WESTERN-STYLE COLE SLAW

MARINADE
1 cup mild-flavored honey
1 cup wine vinegar
1/2 cup finely chopped onion
1 tsp. salt
1 tsp. celery seed

4 cups finely chopped white or red cabbage
1 cup diced green bell pepper

Mix marinade in a small saucepan. Bring to a boil, reduce heat and simmer for 5 minutes. Cool. Pour over vegetables and toss lightly. Cover and refrigerate for several hours or overnight to blend flavors. Makes 8 to 10 servings.

AVOCADO SALAD

MARINADE

½ cup vegetable oil
3 tbs. wine vinegar
3 tbs. lemon juice
½ tsp. sugar
⅛ tsp. salt
⅛ tsp. pepper

2 medium-sized ripe avocados
½ Bermuda onion, sliced paper-thin
1 orange
shredded lettuce

Peel avocados and cut into cubes. Place in a bowl with onion slices. Mix marinade and pour over vegetables. Cover and refrigerate for several hours, stirring occasionally. Just before serving, peel and section orange, add to salad and toss lightly. Serve on a bed of shredded lettuce. Makes 4 servings.

MARINATED EGGPLANT

MARINADE
$\frac{1}{2}$ cup wine vinegar
1 clove garlic, mashed
1 tsp. oregano
1 tsp. salt
$\frac{1}{2}$ tsp. dried basil
$\frac{1}{2}$ tsp. pepper
1 tsp. fresh dill, optional

1 unpeeled eggplant, cut into 1-inch cubes
salted water
$\frac{1}{4}$ cup olive oil

Boil eggplant in salted water to cover until cubes are soft but retain their shape, about 10 minutes. Drain. Combine marinade ingredients and pour marinade over eggplant in a bowl. Cover and refrigerate for 8 hours or overnight. Just before serving, toss with olive oil. Makes 6 to 8 servings.

NOTE: Add the dill if you prefer a Scandinavian flavor.

MUSTARD-HERB TOMATOES

MARINADE

1/4 cup olive oil, or vegetable oil
1 tbs. tarragon vinegar
1 tbs. red wine vinegar
1 clove garlic, crushed
1/4 cup chopped fresh parsley
2 tsp. Dijon-style mustard
1 tsp. salt
1 tsp. sugar
1/4 tsp. pepper

3 large tomatoes, sliced

Cut tomatoes into 1/2-inch slices and restack slices to look like whole tomatoes in a serving dish. Mix marinade ingredients together until well blended and pour over tomatoes. Cover and refrigerate for 2 hours. Let stand at room temperature for 20 minutes before serving. Makes 5 to 6 servings.

NOTE: The tomato slices stacked in this way make an attractive presentation.

STRING BEANS NIÇOISE

MARINADE

2 tbs. wine vinegar	1 tsp. salt
6 tbs. olive oil	½ tsp. coarsley ground black pepper
1 tbs. fresh lemon juice	1 clove garlic, pressed

2 cans (16 oz. each) whole string beans
1 tsp. dried basil
1 tsp. freshly ground pepper
lettuce

Combine marinade ingredients and blend well. Drain beans and spread a layer in an 8-inch square baking dish. Cover with a layer of marinade and sprinkle with basil and pepper. Repeat layers. Cover and refrigerate overnight, turning gently to keep ingredients covered with liquid. Drain excess dressing and serve beans on a bed of lettuce. Makes 4 to 6 servings.

NOTE: If you wish, you may substitute 1 cup prepared French dressing for the marinade in this recipe.

FRENCH-CUT STRING BEANS WITH BACON AND WINE

MARINADE

½ cup cider vinegar
½ cup dry white wine

⅓ cup vegetable oil
½ cup sugar

1 lb. fresh or frozen string beans, cut
  French-style
6 slices bacon

1 medium onion, cut into narrow wedges
1 tsp. Dijon-style mustard
salt and pepper to taste

Prepare beans and cook in lightly salted water until just tender. Drain and place beans in a bowl. Cut bacon crosswise into strips about ⅛-inch wide. Fry in a skillet over moderate heat, stirring frequently, until light brown. Remove bacon from pan. Pour off bacon drippings, leaving just enough to sauté onion wedges. Stir until onion is tender, about 2 to 3 minutes.

Mix marinade ingredients and add to onion in pan. Slowly bring liquid to a boil, scraping bottom of skillet with a wooden spoon. Simmer for 3 minutes. Stir in mustard until well blended. Pour liquid over string beans. Add bacon, salt and pepper. Marinate in the refrigerator overnight. Serve in deep salad bowls. Makes 4 servings.

BASIC THREE-BEAN SALAD

MARINADE

⅔ cup vinegar
⅓ cup vegetable oil
¾ cup sugar

1 tsp. salt
1 tsp. pepper
½ tsp. dried oregano

1 can (16 oz.) cut green beans
1 can (16 oz.) cut wax beans
1 can (16 oz.) kidney beans

1 red or white onion, sliced and
  separated into rings
1 green bell pepper, sliced
lettuce, optional

Drain beans and discard liquid. Rinse kidney beans (or other canned legumes if you use them) with cold water and drain again. Combine beans with onions and green pepper in a bowl. Cover with marinade and refrigerate overnight. To serve, toss to coat well with marinade, drain thoroughly and serve in dishes or on a bed of lettuce. Makes 6 to 8 servings.

NOTE: Garbanzo beans, black beans or other favorites are also good in this salad. Simply replace an equal amount of the other types of beans.

SWEET-SOUR BEETS (INDONESIAN ATJAR BIET)

MARINADE

1 can (10½ oz.) beef bouillon,
OR
1¼ cups bouillon made from
2 bouillon cubes
¾ cup white wine vinegar
2 tbs. sugar
2 tsp. whole cloves
2 tsp. peppercorns

1-1½ cans (1 lb. each) sliced beets, drained

Pour bouillon into a saucepan and add remaining marinade ingredients. Bring to a boil, remove from heat and add beets. Let stand for several hours or overnight. Drain and serve. Makes 4 to 6 servings.

NOTE: You may use fresh beets in this recipe instead of canned. Boil cleaned beets in the spice mixture until tender. Remove the beets and slice them. Return them to the spice mixture and marinate as directed.

CARROTS IN SWEET PICKLE BRINE

MARINADE

1-1½ cups sweet pickle brine, left
over from jar pickles
2 sprigs fresh parsley
1 thin slice fresh lemon

1-2 bunches baby carrots, 3-4 inches long, scrubbed but not peeled
OR
½ lb. packaged baby carrots

Heat pickle brine, parsley and lemon to boiling. Add carrots and simmer for about 5 minutes until carrots are crisp-tender. Cool. Store in the refrigerator in a covered glass container for 4 to 6 hours or until thoroughly chilled. Makes 3 to 4 servings.

NOTE: These pickled carrots make a good addition to an appetizer platter. The next time you finish a jar of sweet pickles, save the brine to make this treat.

NORTH AFRICAN CUCUMBERS

MARINADE
2 tbs. vegetable oil
3 tbs. red wine vinegar
½ tsp. dried thyme
½ tsp. salt
¼ tsp. dried oregano
¼ tsp. dried marjoram

2 large cucumbers, peeled, halved lengthwise, cut into 1-inch pieces
fresh parsley sprigs for garnish
paprika for garnish

Mix marinade. Pour over cucumbers and refrigerate overnight. Drain off marinade. Decorate with parsley and sprinkle with paprika for color. Makes 6 servings.

CUCUMBERS IN DILLED SOUR CREAM

MARINADE

1 part vinegar and 1 part water,
  enough to cover cucumbers
1 tbs. sugar
salt and pepper to taste
2 cups sour cream

2 tbs. lemon juice
2 tbs. tarragon vinegar
½ tsp. fresh dill
2 green onions, finely chopped

3 cucumbers, pared and thinly sliced
1 yellow onion, thinly sliced

Mix vinegar, water, sugar, salt and pepper for a preparatory marinade. Pour over cucumbers and sliced onions and refrigerate for 2 hours. Drain thoroughly. Mix remaining ingredients together and gently stir in drained cucumbers and sliced yellow onion. Chill until ready to serve. This dish may be prepared early in the day. Makes 6 servings.

DANISH CUCUMBERS

MARINADE
1/3 cup white vinegar, white wine or
cider vinegar
1½ tsp. sugar
¼ tsp. pepper

3 large cucumbers, peeled and thinly sliced
1 tbs. salt

Lay cucumbers on a plate and cover with salt. Place another plate on top of cucumbers as a weight. This procedure draws out the liquid. Let stand for 1 hour at room temperature or overnight in the refrigerator. Put cucumbers in a strainer or colander. Drain. Lightly rinse off salt with cold water and drain again. Put cucumbers in a bowl, add marinade and let stand for 2 hours. Makes 6 servings.

LETTUCE, SPINACH AND ORANGE SALAD

MARINADE

3 tbs. vegetable oil
2 tbs. vinegar
2 tbs. corn syrup
1/2 tsp. seasoned salt

1/4 tsp. celery seed
1/4 tsp. dill seed
1/8 tsp. pepper

1 medium head iceberg or romaine lettuce
2 cups spinach leaves
2 tangerines or oranges, peeled and sectioned
1/2 cup sliced onion, separated into rings

Tear lettuce and spinach leaves into bite-sized pieces. Cut each tangerine or orange section in half. Mix marinade and pour over fruit and onion rings in a small bowl and marinate for 30 minutes. Just before serving, pour mixture over greens and toss. Makes 4 servings.

NOTE: For a luncheon salad, add one 15 oz. can of tuna, drained and broken, or 2 cups cooked diced chicken to tangerines and onions before marinating.

NUTTY SALAD

MARINADE
½ cup vinegar
¼ cup vegetable oil, or olive oil
¼ tsp. salt
¼ tsp. pepper
¼ tsp. dried oregano

¼ cup broken walnuts
2 tomatoes, peeled and cut into chunks
1 cucumber, peeled and thinly sliced
1 cup thinly sliced celery

1 onion, sliced and separated into rings
¼ cup sliced green or black olives
shredded lettuce

Mix marinade ingredients thoroughly and pour over nuts and all vegetables except lettuce. Toss well. Cover and refrigerate for 1½ hours, tossing occasionally. Drain before serving or use a slotted spoon and serve salad on a bed of shredded lettuce. Makes 4 to 6 servings.

ZUCCHINI AND MUSHROOMS

MARINADE

1/4 cup vegetable oil
1/3 cup tarragon vinegar
2 tbs. lemon or lime juice
2 tbs. brandy
1 1/4 tsp. onion salt
1/2 tsp. sugar

1/4 tsp. white pepper
1/4 tsp. dried basil
1/8 tsp. fresh dill weed
1/8 tsp. paprika
3 drops hot pepper sauce

1/2 lb. mushrooms, thinly sliced
1/2 lb. small zucchini, thinly sliced
2 tbs. chopped pimiento for garnish
2 tbs. chopped fresh parsley for garnish

Combine marinade ingredients and mix thoroughly in a small jar. Pour over sliced mushrooms and zucchini and mix gently. Chill for 1 hour. Garnish with pimiento and parsley before serving. Makes 6 to 8 servings.

MINTED ZUCCHINI

MARINADE

½ cup vinegar
2 tbs. lemon juice
1 clove garlic, finely chopped
1 tbs. grated onion
1 tbs. chopped fresh mint, or
¼ tsp. mint extract

2 medium zucchini, thinly sliced
1-2 tbs. vegetable oil

Sauté zucchini in oil, turning often until lightly browned. Transfer from skillet to a glass bowl. Cool. Mix marinade and add to zucchini. Chill for at least 1 hour. Makes 4 servings.

LEMON-GARLIC BROCCOLI

MARINADE

½ cup vegetable oil
⅓ cup lemon juice
1 clove garlic, finely chopped
salt and freshly ground
pepper to taste

1 bunch fresh broccoli, about 1 lb.
¼ cup water

Trim broccoli stems and separate into florets. Steam in water until crisp-tender. Drain. Blend marinade and pour over hot broccoli. Cover and refrigerate until well chilled. Serve cold. Makes 4 to 6 servings.

SPINACH MUSHROOM SALAD
WITH MUSTARD MARINADE

MARINADE

1 tbs. prepared mustard
1 tbs. sugar, or mild-flavored honey
1/2 tsp. salt

1/4 tsp. pepper
1/4 cup vinegar
3/4 cup vegetable oil

1/2 lb. fresh spinach
1 small head butter lettuce
1/4 lb. mushrooms, thinly sliced

1/2 green bell pepper, diced
1 hard-cooked egg

Blend mustard, sugar, salt and pepper. Gradually beat in vinegar until well blended. Beat in oil and continue beating until marinade is well blended. Wash, drain and tear spinach and lettuce into bite-sized pieces. Combine mushrooms and green pepper with 1/2 of the marinade and chill for 1 hour or longer. Combine mixture with greens and toss. Add more dressing as needed to moisten. Toss again. Garnish with egg slices or wedges. Makes 4 to 6 servings.

VINAIGRETTE VEGETABLES

MARINADE

1 cup vegetable oil
6 tbs. white wine vinegar
6 tbs. lemon juice

1 tsp. salt
1½ tsp. dry mustard
1 tsp. sugar

2 pt. fresh Brussels sprouts, or 2 pkg. (10 oz. each) frozen Brussels sprouts, halved, cooked until tender
1 head cauliflower, separated into florets, cooked until crisp-tender

1 jar (7 oz.) artichoke hearts, drained
8-10 tomato shells
lettuce
green bell pepper rings and sieved hard-cooked eggs for garnish

Rinse cooked Brussels sprouts and cauliflower in cold water and drain thoroughly. Mix marinade and blend well. Pour marinade over Brussels sprouts, cauliflower and artichoke hearts in a bowl. Cover and refrigerate for at least 2 hours, occasionally spooning marinade over vegetables. To serve, remove vegetables with a slotted spoon, or drain marinade and spoon vegetables into tomato shells on lettuce leaves for individual salad servings. Garnish with green pepper rings and sieved hard-cooked eggs. Makes 8 to 10 servings.

PICKLED CABBAGE

MARINADE-PICKLING SOLUTION
2½ cups white wine vinegar
1 tbs. soft butter
1 tbs. pickling spices

2 lb. Chinese cabbage or napa cabbage, cut crosswise into 1-inch slices
1½ cups water
½ cup kosher salt, or other coarse salt

Combine cabbage, water and salt in a large bowl and let stand at room temperature for 1 hour. Drain, pressing out excess liquid.

Combine cabbage and marinade ingredients in a large bowl. Pack cabbage and marinade mixture into two 1-quart jars. Refrigerate, covered, for at least 4 days. Pickled cabbage may be stored, covered tightly, in the refrigerator for about 3 weeks. For longer storage use canning procedures, which can be found in comprehensive cookbooks under canning/pickling, or in specialized cookbooks on canning. Makes 8 to 10 servings.

HAWAIIAN-STYLE PICKLED ONIONS

MARINADE-PICKLING SOLUTION
4 cups white wine vinegar
1 cup sugar
1 tbs. coarse salt
dash cayenne pepper

2 lb. small white Texas or Spanish onions
4 cups water
1 tbs. salt

Add onions to water and salt in a bowl, cover and refrigerate overnight. Drain onions and rinse under cold running water. Heat marinade ingredients in a large saucepan to boiling; simmer for 3 minutes. Pack into hot sterilized jars and refrigerate, covered, until cold. May be stored for about 3 months. Makes 10 to 12 servings.

PICKLED RED ONIONS

MARINADE-PICKLING SOLUTION

2 cloves garlic, sliced
10 peppercorns
1/4 tsp. dried oregano
1/2 tsp. salt
3/4 cup vinegar (or enough to cover
onion in a 1-pint jar)

1 large red onion (about 1/2 lb.), thinly sliced

Place onion in a jar with spices and add vinegar to cover. Cover jar and store in a cool place for 2 to 3 days before using. Makes 2 to 4 servings.

MEXICAN-STYLE PICKLED ONION RINGS

MARINADE-PICKLING SOLUTION
1 cup vinegar
1 tsp. salt
$\frac{1}{8}$ tsp. dried oregano
1 dried red chile, broken
into small pieces, or 1 tsp. cayenne
pepper

boiling water
4 medium onions, thinly sliced and separated into rings

Pour boiling water over onion rings and drain through a colander. Combine onion rings and mixed marinade ingredients in a 1-quart jar. Cover and marinate for at least 1 hour before using. Makes 10 to 12 servings.

BEEF ENTRÉES

With marinades, less costly, tougher cuts of meat can be made tender and tantalizing. A blade pot roast, steeped in a peppery marinade for several hours, will have a zippy chile-flavored bite. A standard-grade meat can taste like a choice cut when soaked in an herbed red wine marinade overnight. Or meat from a bony cut can be trimmed away, cubed and soaked in a tangy spiced solution for skewering and broiling as a kabob.

Marinades must be treated with respect and common sense. When properly used, they enhance flavor and tenderize without being overpowering. It is important to consider the characteristics of the foods and estimate the length of time for marinating.

Beef, lamb, veal, pork, game, poultry and fish can all be marinated, but their characteristics differ. A thick, tough cut of red meat will take longer to absorb the flavors of the marinade than will a delicate fish or chicken. The recipes in this chapter have all been tested, but they can vary with individual cuts of beef from different parts of the country. So some experimentation is suggested.

It is not necessary to cover completely large cuts of meat or chicken with the marinade. They can be placed with the marinade in a locking food storage bag or other container and turned frequently so all surfaces eventually absorb the marinade. Most meats marinate well in 1 hour at room temperature and 6 hours in the refrigerator. *Do not marinate meat longer than 1 hour at room temperature of about 70° because of potential bacterial growth.* The tougher and larger the cut of meat, the longer the marinating time. Very large cuts may require 24 to 48 hours. Roasts and other thick cuts should be pierced to the center with a skewer or knife blade so that the marinade can penetrate and tenderize all the way through.

With each type of entrée, basic marinades are offered that you can use with any cooking method you desire — roasting, baking or grilling. The same marinades used for steaks and roasts can be used for hamburger, but a hamburger patty requires only about 3 hours of marinating in the refrigerator.

GENERAL DIRECTIONS FOR MARINATING STEAK OR HAMBURGER

Prepare ¾ to 1 cup liquid to marinate about 1½ to 2 pounds steak, since the meat does not have to be immersed completely. Steak should be turned once during the minimum marinating time of 2 hours at room temperature or 4 hours in the refrigerator. The same marinades may be used for roasts.

Double the amount of liquid for a 3- to 5-pound roast. The marinade should reach about ⅔ up the height of the roast, so place roasts in a deep bowl to marinate. Pierce meat deeply with a skewer in three or four places to allow marinade to penetrate.

After marinating, drain off the liquid and use it for basting and to make sauce or gravy. **Be sure to boil reserved marinade for at least 3 minutes before using.** Broil or grill steaks and hamburgers, or bake hamburgers, allowing about 30 minutes at 350°.

GARLIC AND SOUR CREAM ON STEAK

MARINADE

1 cup sour cream
1 tbs. lemon juice
2 cloves garlic, crushed
$\frac{1}{4}$ tsp. pepper
$\frac{1}{4}$ tsp. celery salt
$\frac{1}{2}$ tsp. salt
$\frac{1}{2}$ tsp. paprika
1 tsp. Worcestershire sauce

2-3 lb. steak, or hamburger

Combine ingredients and marinate steak, covered, overnight in the refrigerator. Drain meat and cook, using the method of your choice (see page 65). Makes 4 to 6 servings.

NOTE: The same marinade is also delicious when used with chicken.

TERIYAKI MARINADE FOR BEEF

MARINADE

2 tbs. vegetable oil
2 tbs. sugar
2 tbs. sherry, or dry white wine
1 tbs. soy sauce
½ cup beef stock (canned or made
from bouillon cube)
1 clove garlic, pressed
1 piece (about ⅛ inch) ginger root,
minced, or 4 tsp. ground ginger
salt and pepper to taste

2-3 lb. steak, or hamburger

Marinate meat in the refrigerator for 4 to 6 hours or overnight. Drain meat and cook, using the method of your choice (see page 65). Makes 4 to 6 servings.

SHERRY MARINADE FOR BEEF

MARINADE
½ cup dry sherry
¼ cup vegetable oil
¼ cup olive oil
1 medium onion, finely chopped
1 clove garlic, minced
1 tbs. chopped fresh parsley
½ tsp. salt

2-3 lb. steak, or hamburger

Mix ingredients and pour over meat. Marinate in the refrigerator for 2 to 10 hours. Drain meat and cook, using the method of your choice (see page 65). Makes 4 to 6 servings.

FAT-FREE WINE MARINADE FOR BEEF

MARINADE

¾ cup tarragon vinegar, wine
vinegar or wine
1 medium onion, minced
½ cup chopped fresh parsley
1½ tsp. minced garlic
½ tsp. dried thyme, or cumin
1 bay leaf, crushed
3 drops hot pepper sauce, or
dash dried red pepper flakes

2-3 lb. steak or hamburgers

Combine all ingredients. Marinate meat in the refrigerator for 2 to 4 hours. Drain meat and cook, using the method of your choice (see page 65). Makes 4 to 6 servings.

FAT-FREE BROTH MARINADE FOR BEEF

MARINADE

1 cup beef broth, made with 1
bouillon cube
2 tbs. cider vinegar
2 tbs. soy sauce
2 cloves garlic, crushed
2 tbs. chopped fresh parsley
salt and pepper to taste

2-3 lb. steak, or hamburger

Mix all ingredients. Marinate for 30 minutes at room temperature or 3 hours in the refrigerator. Drain meat and cook, using the method of your choice (see page 65). Makes 1 cup.

ROUND STEAK IN BEER MARINADE

MARINADE
¼ cup brown sugar, firmly packed
2 tbs. prepared German-style mustard
1 tbs. vinegar
½ tsp. salt
¼ tsp. coarsely ground pepper
1 cup beer
1 medium onion, chopped
1 bay leaf

1 top round steak, about 1¼ inches thick

Combine brown sugar, mustard, vinegar, salt and pepper in a saucepan. Heat and slowly stir in beer. Add onion and bay leaf and continue to cook over low heat for 10 minutes, stirring occasionally. Cool. Place steak in a flat dish. Add marinade and turn meat to coat. Cover dish and refrigerate for 6 to 8 hours or overnight, turning meat at least once. Drain marinade and grill or broil steak. Cut into thin slices to serve. Makes 4 to 6 servings.

ITALIAN ROUND STEAK

MARINADE
1 cup prepared Italian dressing
$\frac{1}{2}$ cup red wine
1 tbs. Worcestershire sauce

2-2$\frac{1}{2}$ lb. round steak, about 1$\frac{1}{2}$ inches thick

Combine marinade ingredients and marinate steak for 6 hours or overnight. Drain and grill or broil meat. Slice diagonally across the grain to serve. Makes 4 to 6 servings.

PORTERHOUSE STEAK
WITH ZESTY WINE MARINADE

MARINADE
½ cup red Burgundy wine, or
⅓ cup bottled steak sauce
3 tbs. lemon juice
2 tbs. vegetable oil
1½ tsp. sugar
½ tsp. seasoning salt
¼ tsp. pepper

1 porterhouse steak, about 1½ inches thick, about 4 lb.

Combine marinade ingredients and pour over steak. Marinate for 4 hours in the refrigerator, turning meat occasionally. Drain and broil or grill. Makes 8 to 10 servings.

FLANK STEAK WITH ROSÉ WINE

MARINADE

¾ cup rosé wine
¼ cup vegetable oil
1 large clove garlic, crushed
½ tsp. salt
1 tsp. pepper

1 flank steak, about 2 lb.

Mix marinade and pour over meat. Turn meat to coat and place in the refrigerator, covered, for 3 to 4 hours. Drain and broil or grill. Thinly slice meat diagonally across the grain to serve. Boil remaining marinade for at least 3 minutes and use for sauce. Makes 4 to 5 servings.

MEXICAN STEAK

MARINADE
2 tbs. olive oil
¼ cup orange juice
¼ cup tomato juice
2 tbs. lime juice
1 tsp. paprika
1 tsp. cumin seed
1 tsp. drled oregano
½ tsp. dried red pepper flakes
2 tsp. minced garlic

3 lb. sirloin or porterhouse steak, 2 inches thick

Mix marinade ingredients and pour over steak. Cover and refrigerator for 6 hours or overnight. Drain and broil or grill steak. Makes 6 to 8 servings.

SOUTHERN-STYLE LONDON BROIL

MARINADE
1 can (8 oz.) tomato sauce
2 tbs. bourbon, or gin
2 tbs. chopped chives
1/4 tsp. minced garlic
1/4 tsp. salt
1/4 tsp. celery salt
1/2 tsp. pepper

1 London broil, or thickly cut flank steak
1/4 lb. mushrooms, sautéed

Combine marinade ingredients and pour over steak and mushrooms. Marinate for 3 to 4 hours in the refrigerator, turning meat occasionally. Drain, setting aside marinade and mushrooms. Broil or grill meat. Heat marinade mixture and mushrooms to just under boiling. Slice steak across the grain and serve with mushroom-marinade sauce. Makes 4 servings.

KOREAN-STYLE BARBECUED BEEF

> **MARINADE**
>
> 1/3 cup vegetable oil
> 1/3 cup soy sauce
> 1/4 cup sugar
> 1/4 cup minced green onions
> 3 cloves garlic, minced
> 2 tbs. toasted sesame seeds*
> dash hot pepper sauce
> 1/2 tsp. salt

1 1/2 lb. boneless beef round, sirloin tip or chuck steak,
cut into serving-sized pieces

Mix marinade and pour over beef. Marinate for 4 to 6 hours or overnight in the refrigerator. Drain marinade and grill meat. Heat marinade for sauce. Makes 3 to 4 servings.

*Toast sesame seeds in a 350° oven for 10 minutes, stirring frequently to prevent burning, or over medium heat in a dry skillet, stirring until browned.

JAPANESE-STYLE STEAK

MARINADE

⅓ cup sake, or dry sherry
⅓ cup soy sauce
¼ cup sugar
1½ tsp. grated ginger root, or ½ tsp.
ground ginger
¼ clove garlic, minced
¼ lemon, thinly sliced

1 lb. lean sirloin or porterhouse steak, cut into thin strips

Add meat slices to combined marinade ingredients. Marinate for about 15 minutes and drain. Cook steak slices briefly in a hot skillet. Makes 4 servings.

STEAK ORIENTALE WITH ITALIAN DRESSING

MARINADE
1 cup prepared Italian salad dressing
¼ cup soy sauce
2 tbs. brown sugar

2-2½ lb. steak of your choice, about 1-1½ inches thick
1 green bell pepper, cut into chunks
1 onion, sliced

Mix marinade and add steak. Cover and marinate in the refrigerator for 4 hours or overnight, turning occasionally. Broil and brush with marinade. Broil green pepper and onion during last 10 minutes. Makes 4 to 6 servings.

BEEF ROAST WITH ORANGE FLAVOR

MARINADE

½ cup dry red wine
½ cup vegetable oil
⅓ cup soy sauce
⅓ cup frozen orange juice concentrate,
  thawed

1 tsp. grated ginger root, or ¼ tsp.
  ground ginger
1 clove garlic, minced

3-4 lb. rump, chuck, eye, or other roast

Pierce roast. Combine marinade ingredients. Pour over roast and marinate in the refrigerator overnight. Turn several times while marinating. Remove meat from refrigerator about 2 hours before roasting and drain. Preheat oven to 550°. Put roast in oven, immediately reduce heat to 350° and roast for 18 to 20 minutes per pound, or until meat reaches an internal temperature between 140°(rare)* and 170° (well done). Makes 8 to 10 servings.

*Health authorities discourage the eating of undercooked beef because of possible bacterial contamination.

SPANISH-STYLE PRIME RIB ROAST

MARINADE

1 cup wine vinegar	1 crumbled bay leaf
1/2 cup Burgundy wine	1/2 tsp. dried tarragon
1/2 cup water	3 drops hot pepper sauce, or 1/4 tsp.
2 tbs. gin	dried red pepper flakes
1 tbs. onion juice	1/2 tbs. salt
1 clove garlic, crushed	

4 lb. rib eye or prime rib roast

Mix marinade and pour over meat in a shallow pan. Marinate in the refrigerator overnight. Turn occasionally. Return to room temperature before roasting. Roast at 300° until done to your taste, using a meat thermometer (see directions page 80). Baste with marinade every 1/2 hour. Makes 8 servings.

SEVEN-BONE CHUCK ROAST

MARINADE

1 cup ketchup
½ cup water
¼ cup wine vinegar
2 tbs. dry onion soup mix

2 tbs. Worcestershire sauce
1 tbs. brown sugar
1 tbs. prepared mustard
1 tsp. chili powder

one 7-bone chuck roast, about 5 lb.
unseasoned meat tenderizer

Sprinkle beef with tenderizer, following label directions. Combine marinade ingredients and bring to a boil. Pour marinade over beef and coat all sides. Marinate for at least 1 hour in the refrigerator. Drain. Roast according to directions on page 80, basting frequently. Boil reserved marinade for at least 3 minutes and serve as a sauce over sliced roast.

MALAYSIAN HAMBURGERS

MARINADE

4 fresh mild chiles, seeded
1 dried red chile, broken into pieces
2 small onions, minced
½ tsp. minced ginger root
¼ cup lemon juice

1 tbs. brown sugar
pinch saffron or turmeric
1½ cups coconut milk
¼ tsp. salt

1-2 lb. lean ground beef, or chopped sirloin,
shaped as small meat loaves or flattened hamburgers

With a mortar and pestle, crush fresh and dried chiles. Mix into a paste with onions, ginger and lemon juice. Or add chiles, onions (quartered) and ginger root with lemon juice to the work bowl of a food processor and process until blended into a paste. Add sugar, saffron or turmeric, salt and coconut milk. Blend. Pour over meat and marinate in the refrigerator for 4 hours, turning meat frequently. Drain. Bake in a 350° oven for ½ hour, or broil or grill. Boil remaining marinade for at least 3 minutes and use for sauce. Makes 4 to 8 servings.

PROVENÇAL BEEF STEW

MARINADE
½ cup cognac
½ cup orange juice
3 cups red wine

4 lb. stewing beef, cut into 1½-inch cubes
2 lb. large eggplant
2½ cups chopped onions
¼ cup olive oil
½ lb. sliced bacon, diced
1 pt. cherry tomatoes, or 4 medium tomatoes, chopped
1 can (10½ oz.) beef bouillon
3 cloves garlic, minced
4 sprigs fresh parsley, chopped
2 bay leaves
2 pieces orange rind, about ½-inch wide and 3 inches long
4 cloves
¼ cup tomato paste

Mix marinade and combine with beef in a large bowl. Marinate for 6 hours or longer. Remove meat with a slotted spoon and dry on paper towels. Reserve marinade. Dice eggplant and soak in salted water for 30 minutes.

Preheat oven to 350°. Cook onions in oil until tender. Remove onions with a slotted spoon and set aside. Brown bacon and set aside. Brown drained eggplant thoroughly and set aside. Cherry tomatoes may be sautéed briefly and set aside. Brown beef and combine with bacon and onion in a 3-quart casserole. Add reserved marinade, beef bouillon, garlic, parsley, bay leaves, orange rind and cloves. Bake, covered, for 1½ hours or until tender. Stir in tomato paste. Add cherry tomatoes and eggplant and cook for 10 minutes longer. Remove bay leaves before serving. Makes 10 to 12 servings.

SZECHWAN SHREDDED BEEF

> **MARINADE**
> 1 tsp. light soy sauce
> 1 tbs. sherry
> ½ egg white, beaten slightly

¾ lb. partially frozen flank steak, shredded or cut into very thin strips
3 tbs. peanut or safflower oil
1 clove garlic, minced
½ tbs. minced ginger root
½ cup grated carrot
½ fresh red chili pepper, cut into thin strips, or 1 dried red chili pepper,
broken into pieces
½ cup red bell pepper, cut into thin strips
2 cups snow peas, ends trimmed, strings removed, cut into thin strips
4 scallions, white part only, cut into thin strips lengthwise

SEASONING SAUCE

1 tbs. hoisin sauce

1 tbs. bean sauce

1 tbs. sherry

1 tbs. Chinese red vinegar

1 tbs. dark soy sauce

2 tsp. plum sauce

1 tsp. hot pepper sauce

Mix marinade and add shredded beef. Cover and refrigerate at least 30 minutes and up to 12 hours.

Mix all seasoning sauce ingredients together in a bowl. Arrange all remaining ingredients except oil on a tray in preparation for stir-frying. Heat a wok or electric frying pan to medium heat. Add 1 tbs. oil and heat for 20 seconds until hot but not smoking. Add garlic and ginger and stir-fry for 15 seconds. Add carrot and stir-fry for 1 minute. Raise heat to high and add hot and sweet peppers, snow peas and scallions; stir-fry for 1 minute. Transfer all contents of wok with a slotted spoon to a heated serving dish.

Add remaining oil to wok and turn heat to high. Stir-fry marinated meat in wok until it loses its redness, about 2 minutes. Stir seasoning sauce again and add to wok with beef. Return vegetables to work. Stir-fry rapidly for 1 more minute, mixing ingredients gently but thoroughly. Transfer to a heated serving dish and serve at once.

Makes 2 to 3 servings as an entrée, 4 to 6 servings with other Chinese dishes.

SPICY MEXICAN BEEF JERKY

MARINADE

2 tbs. water

2 tbs. Worcestershire sauce

1 tsp. salt

1 tsp. cumin

2 cloves garlic, pressed

1½ tsp. chili powder

⅛ tsp. cayenne pepper

1-1½ lb. boneless beef top round steak, flank steak, chuck or other steak

Trim all fat from meat and discard. Slice meat ⅛-inch thick and make slices as long as possible, either with or across the grain.*

Combine marinade ingredients in a bowl, stir well and add meat slices. Mix thoroughly and refrigerate overnight. Drain meat. Shake off excess liquid and discard marinade. Arrange strips of meat close together but not overlapping on a broiler rack set in a foil-lined, rimmed baking or broiling pan to catch drips.

Bake uncovered in a 200° oven for 5 to 6 hours or until meat feels dry and is dark brown. Pat off any remaining oil with a paper towel. Cool. Remove from racks and store in airtight containers in the freezer.

*If you partially freeze the meat before preparation, it will be easier to slice into the narrow strips

required, or have your butcher slice it for you. Cut meat across the grain for a tender, slightly brittle jerky. Cut with the grain if you like it chewier.

NOTE: Marinated dried meats make delicious high-protein snacks and appetizers. To be absolutely safe, store homemade beef jerky in the freezer to avoid bacterial growth.

HAWAIIAN BEEF JERKY (PIPI KAULA)

MARINADE	
1/4 cup soy sauce	2 tbs. minced ginger root
1/4 cup dry sherry	1 clove garlic, minced
1 small onion, minced	1 1/2 tsp. coarse salt

1-1 1/2 lb. boneless beef top round steak, flank steak, chuck or other steak

Trim all fat from meat and discard. Cut into 1/2-inch-thick strips, 4 inches x 1 inch, and pound with a mallet to tenderize.

Combine marinade ingredients in a bowl, stir well and add meat slices. Marinate and bake as directed for *Spicy Mexican Beef Jerky*, page 88.

FRENCH HOT DOGS

MARINADE

1 cup water
3 tbs. lemon juice
1 envelope (1-cup serving) dry onion
  soup mix

1 envelope (1-cup serving) dry
  tomato soup mix
½ tsp. dry mustard

8 beef (or pork and beef) frankfurters
1 tbs. flour

8 French bread rolls
4 tbs. grated Parmesan cheese

Score frankfurters diagonally. Mix marinade ingredients and heat in a skillet, stirring constantly, until it boils. Remove from heat and add frankfurters. Let stand, covered, for 15 to 20 minutes. Remove frankfurters from marinade. Broil or grill 4 inches from heat for 7 to 10 minutes, turning frequently. While frankfurters cook, stir flour into marinade and reheat to boiling, stirring until thick. Serve in French rolls. Spoon marinade over frankfurters and sprinkle with Parmesan cheese. Makes 8 servings.

LAMB, VEAL AND PORK ENTRÉES

Herbs and spices, wines, flavored liqueurs, mustards, and fruit-flavored jellies and jams are the sparkling, taste-appealing ingredients used in the marinades for lamb, veal and pork in recipes from various countries. Such recipes are easy to emulate and fun to prepare because of the delicious results.

Veal is the meat of a young cow that has been carefully fed to produce very tender meat. Choice veal is delicate and tasty without additives, but some veal chops and shoulder cuts can be given interesting flavors with different marinades, and a Mexican version is offered here.

Pork, available in a wide variety of cuts, is a perfect food for marinating. Whether your favorite cuts are pork chops, shoulder or spareribs, the choice of marinades will allow you to experiment until you find the combinations for the flavors you prefer.

These recipes for lamb, veal and pork may be baked, broiled or grilled. When you decide on a basic marinade, select the method of cooking from any one of the other recipes suggesting heat and time. Allow about 1/2 cup marinade for each pound of lamb, veal or pork.

MINT MARINADE FOR LAMB

MARINADE
½ cup water
1 tbs. cider vinegar
1 cup orange or clover honey
⅓ cup minced fresh mint, or ¼ cup
dried mint flakes

3-4 lb. lamb, any cut

Bring water and vinegar to a boil. Add honey and stir until dissolved. Remove from heat and stir in mint. Cool. Marinate for 3 to 4 hours in the refrigerator. Use to marinate any lamb cuts for broiling or barbecuing. Makes about 1¾ cups, or enough for 8 to 10 servings.

ARMENIAN HERB MARINADE FOR LAMB

MARINADE

½ cup olive oil, or vegetable oil
½ cup tomato juice
½ cup finely chopped onion
¼ cup lemon juice
¼ cup snipped fresh parsley

1 clove garlic, minced
1 tsp. salt
1 tsp. dried marjoram
1 tsp. dried thyme
½ tsp. pepper

3-4 lb. lamb, any cut

Combine all ingredients and pour marinade mixture over lamb cuts to be broiled or barbecued. Marinate in a covered dish in the refrigerator for 6 hours or overnight. Be sure to turn meat in marinade so all sides are coated. Makes about 1¾ cups, or enough for 8 to 10 servings.

NOTE: This recipe may also be used for pork and chicken.

FAT-FREE SPICE MARINADE FOR LAMB

MARINADE

1 cup wine vinegar
1 onion, chopped
8 whole cloves
2 sprigs fresh mint, or 1 tsp. dried
2 cloves garlic, crushed

4 sprigs fresh parsley, or 1 tsp. dried
1/8 tsp. dried thyme
1/8 tsp. dried tarragon
1 tsp. grated lemon rind
1/2 tsp. salt

1 lb. lamb, any cut

Mix all ingredients and pour over lamb. Marinate for 3 to 4 hours in the refrigerator. Drain marinade and cook as desired. Makes 1 cup for 1 or 2 servings of lamb chops or other lamb cuts.

LAMB CHOPS L'ORANGE

MARINADE

½ cup orange juice, or ¼ cup frozen
orange juice concentrate, thawed
3 tbs. soy sauce
2 tsp. sugar
1 tsp. minced garlic
1 tsp. ground ginger
⅛ tsp. pepper

6 shoulder lamb chops, ¾-inch thick
2 oranges, cut into 6 wedges each
1-2 tbs. cornstarch

Arrange chops in a flat glass baking dish. Combine marinade ingredients, pour over chops, cover and refrigerate for 2 hours. Cover and bake with marinade at 350° for 1 hour or until tender. Transfer chops to a serving plate and garnish with orange wedges. Skim fat from drippings; thicken drippings with 1 tbs. cornstarch per cup of juice. Spoon over meat and oranges. Makes 6 servings.

PORTUGUESE-STYLE LAMB CHOPS

MARINADE

½ cup vegetable oil
¼ cup rosé wine
1 small onion, sliced
1 clove garlic, chopped
1 tbs. Dijon-style mustard
½ tsp. salt
⅛ tsp. pepper

6 shoulder lamb chops, ¾-inch thick

Mix marinade ingredients and pour over chops arranged in a flat baking dish, covering both sides evenly. Cover and refrigerate for 8 hours. Drain marinade and reserve to use for basting during cooking. Broil or grill until tender. Chops may be baked uncovered in a 350° oven for 50 to 60 minutes. Baste often with marinade. Makes 6 servings.

MINTED LEG OF LAMB

> ### MARINADE
> ½ cup vegetable oil
> 1 cup dry white wine, or dry vermouth
> 2 garlic cloves, crushed
> 1 tsp. dried mint flakes, crushed, or
> 3 fresh mint leaves
> ½ tsp. dried orange peel, or 1½ tsp.
> freshly grated peel
> ½ tsp. salt
> ¼ tsp. pepper

1 leg of lamb, about 3-4 lb., boned and butterflied

Have the butcher bone and butterfly lamb so it can be laid out flat for broiling. Mix marinade ingredients and pour over lamb in a covered dish. Marinate in the refrigerator overnight. Turn several times. Drain. Broil or grill until browned on both sides and a meat thermometer in thickest part registers about 140° to 150°. Makes 6 to 8 servings.

STUFFED LEG OF LAMB

MARINADE

1 cup dry white wine
1 tbs. vegetable oil

1 can frozen pineapple-grapefruit juice
concentrate, mixed with 1½ cups
water, divided

---

1 leg of lamb, boned
½ tsp. salt
½ fruit juice mixture used in marinade
2 grated apples

½ cup breadcrumbs
½ tsp. dried rosemary
1 tsp. crushed fresh mint
2 tbs. butter

Spread lamb and salt interior. Combine ½ juice mixture with apples, breadcrumbs, rosemary, mint and butter; spread over inside of meat. Roll lamb back into original leg shape and tie with twine. Mix wine, vegetable oil and ½ fruit juice mixture; pour over meat in a roasting pan. Cover and refrigerate overnight, turning occasionally. Drain and reserve marinade. Roast meat on a rack in a roasting pan at 450° for 15 minutes; reduce heat to 325° and roast for about 2 hours or until tender. Baste frequently with marinade. Skim off fat and thicken pan juices (use 1 tbs. cornstarch per 1 cup juice) for gravy. Makes 6 to 8 servings.

MEXICAN-STYLE BARBECUED VEAL CHOPS

MARINADE

½ cup cider vinegar
¼ cup vegetable oil
¼ cup ketchup
½ cup minced onion
1 clove garlic, minced

½ tsp. dried thyme
½ tsp. ground cumin
½ tsp. chili powder
¼ tsp. cayenne pepper
1½ tsp. salt

6 veal chops, 1½ inches thick, rinsed and dried

Combine marinade ingredients and add chops. Marinate in the refrigerator for 6 hours. Drain chops and broil 5 inches from heat for 15 to 20 minutes or until brown. Baste with marinade during cooking. Makes 6 servings.

LEMON MARINADE FOR VEAL

MARINADE

¾ cup wine vinegar
3 tbs. lemon juice
1 medium onion, minced
1 clove garlic, crushed
1 bay leaf, crumbled

¼ cup chopped fresh parsley
⅛ tsp. dried thyme
⅛ tsp. dried tarragon
2 tsp. salt
½ tsp. pepper

2 lb. veal, any cut

Marinate veal in the refrigerator for a minimum of 4 hours. Drain and cook as desired. Makes about 1 cup marinade.

SPICE SEASONING MIX FOR PORK

SEASONING MIX

2 tbs. crumbled bay leaves	2 tbs. dried thyme
2 tbs. ground cloves	2 tbs. dried basil
2 tbs. mace	2 tbs. cinnamon
2 tbs. nutmeg	2 tbs. dried savory, or parsley
2 tbs. paprika	5 tbs. white pepper

If you cook pork frequently, you may wish to prepare this special seasoning mix to add to other marinade ingredients. The spice mix can be used with any combination of acid and oil in place of, or in addition to, those suggested in recipes for pork. The spice mix may be used for pork roasts, pork chops, barbecued ribs, ham slices and patés, whether or not you are marinating them.

For any spices not already ground or crushed, you can use a spice grinder or electric blender. Mix ingredients and store in an airtight jar on the spice shelf.

CURRIED MARINADE FOR SPARERIBS

MARINADE

¼ cup soy sauce
3 tbs. lemon juice
2 tbs. sherry
1 tsp. curry powder
2 garlic cloves, minced

1½ tsp. instant tea dissolved in 1½ cups
  water, or 1½ cups very strong tea
1 tbs. *Spice Seasoning Mix for Pork*,
  page 102
¼ tsp. hot pepper sauce

4 lb. lean pork ribs
1 tbs. prepared mustard mixed with 1 tbs. honey

Strip membrane from back of ribs. If ribs are fatty, drop them in boiling water for about 5 minutes before marinating. Remove from water and wipe dry with paper towels. Place ribs in a shallow pan. Combine marinade ingredients and pour over ribs. Cover and marinate in the refrigerator for at least 2 hours or overnight, turning so both sides soak in the liquid. Drain and reserve marinade to use for basting. For a final glaze, mix a little mustard with honey and brush on ribs.

To roast: Place ribs on racks in shallow pans and roast at 350° for 1¼ hours.

To grill: Place on grill 3 inches from low heat. Cook about 1¼ hours, turning every 15 minutes. Makes 4 servings.

MUSTARD MARINADE FOR SPARERIBS

MARINADE

½ cup cider vinegar
½ cup chili sauce
½ cup ketchup
2 tbs. lemon juice
1 tbs. Worcestershire sauce
3 tbs. brown sugar

2 tsp. dry mustard
1 garlic clove, finely chopped
½ cup chopped green onion
1 tsp. *Spice Seasoning Mix for Pork,*
 page 102
1 tsp. salt

4-6 lb. lean pork spareribs

Prepare and cook spareribs according to directions on page 103. For this marinade, mix ingredients and marinate spareribs for 2 to 3 hours. Makes about 2 cups marinade for 4 to 6 lb. ribs.

TERIYAKI MARINADE FOR SPARERIBS

MARINADE

½ cup soy sauce
¼ cup dry wine
2 tbs. wine vinegar
2 tbs. honey
2 tsp. ground ginger
1 large clove garlic, crushed
1 tsp. *Spice Seasoning Mix for Pork*,
page 102

2-3 lb. lean pork spareribs

Prepare and cook spareribs according to directions on page 103. For this marinade, mix ingredients and marinate ribs for 2 hours or longer. Makes about 1 cup marinade for 2 to 3 lb. ribs.

COOKED MARINADE FOR PORK

MARINADE

3 cups water
1 cup red wine vinegar
2 onions, chopped
1 carrot, chopped
2 celery stalks, chopped
3 tbs. chopped fresh parsley
2 tbs. *Spice Seasoning Mix for Pork*,
page 102

5-6 lb. pork, any cut

Place all ingredients in a pot and bring to a boil. Simmer for 1 hour. Cool thoroughly. Marinate pork in mixture for at least 3 hours in the refrigerator. Do not use marinade for basting. Makes about 3 cups for approximately 5 to 6 lb. meat.

NOTE: This marinade is also tasty with game, beef and lamb.

DRY MARINADE FOR PORK

MARINADE

2 garlic cloves, peeled
2 tsp. salt
2 tbs. *Spice Seasoning Mix for Pork*,
page 102
2 tbs. grated lemon or orange rind

Use a mortar and pestle, or the back of a spoon in a small bowl, to crush garlic with salt until mixture is like a puree. Add remaining ingredients and mash together. Pierce meat in several places with a fork or skewer and rub marinade into holes and over surface of meat. Place in a covered dish in the refrigerator and marinate for about 6 hours. Prepare pork by any baking, broiling or frying method.

PORK BLADE STEAKS IN BEER

MARINADE
1 cup beer
1 cup bottled barbecue sauce
½ cup chopped onion
1 tsp. *Spice Seasoning Mix for Pork*,
page 102
⅛ tsp. minced garlic

4-6 pork blade steaks, cut ½-¾ inches thick

Combine marinade ingredients. Marinate steaks in mixture in the refrigerator, covered, for about 4 hours, turning steaks several times. Remove steaks from marinade and grill over medium heat for 20 minutes on one side. Brush with marinade and grill other side until done, about 10 minutes on second side for a ½-inch steak and about 15 minutes for a ¾-inch steak. Makes 4 to 6 servings.

BARBECUED HAM STEAKS

MARINADE
4 cups dry sherry
½ cup melted butter, or margarine
4 tsp. ground cloves
4 tsp. paprika
½ cup brown sugar
½ tsp. dry mustard
8 garlic cloves, finely chopped

6 ham steaks, about 1-inch thick

Combine marinade ingredients and marinate ham steaks in mixture for 3 hours in the refrigerator, turning once. Broil or grill. Turn frequently and baste with marinade. Makes 6 servings.

POULTRY ENTRÉES

Chicken is infinite in its variety, with a new taste in store for each marinade. Chicken breasts soaked in a soy sauce marinade become a teriyaki chicken that would do any exotic Oriental cook proud. Add an orange flavor and, voila! You are a French chef extraordinaire! With a little pineapple and lemon juice, you can almost imagine a grass-skirted hula dancer. Many of the recipes in this chapter are designed to add color to the chicken to make it attractive and appetizing. Use prepared French and Italian dressings to make it even easier. There is a whole world of ethnic recipes, too, and you will find several in this chapter.

Cook your marinated chickens any way you like: roast them covered and brown uncovered for the last 15 minutes; bake them uncovered and baste frequently; or grill, broil, fry, microwave or stew.

Marinate a whole chicken or parts. Chicken should be well thawed and patted dry. Remove the skin if you choose. Pierce parts with a fork so the marinade flavors can penetrate the meat and tenderize it. Figure approximately ½ cup marinade per pound of chicken or ¾ cup to 1 cup for a small chicken or the equivalent of 2 whole chicken breasts. Marinate chicken in marinade-safe containers in 1 or 2 layers and turn the chicken parts so the skin side is down once or twice during the marinating time, usually for a minimum of 2 hours. Some recipes call for baking the chicken in the marinade; for others, you pour off the liquid and use it for basting and thickening for a delectable sauce.

LIME-FLAVORED MARINADE FOR CHICKEN

MARINADE

3 tbs. vegetable oil
½ cup lime juice
1 tbs. grated lime peel

¼ tsp. salt
¼ tsp. pepper
(Makes about ⅔ cup for 1 small chicken)

CHILI SAUCE MARINADE FOR CHICKEN

MARINADE

1 cup chili sauce
¼ cup red wine vinegar
½ tbs. horseradish

1 clove garlic, minced
½ tsp. seasoning salt
(Makes 1½ cups for 1 to 2 chickens)

for each recipe:

1 small chicken, or 2 chicken breasts

Mix ingredients together and marinate chicken in the refrigerator for a minimum of 2 hours. Drain chicken and cook as desired.

GREEN ONION AND SOY SAUCE MARINADE FOR CHICKEN

MARINADE
½ cup soy sauce
½ cup thinly sliced green onions
2 tbs. dry sherry
2 tbs. brown sugar
½ tsp. salt

1 small chicken, or 2 chicken breasts

Mix ingredients together and marinate chicken in the refrigerator for a minimum of 2 hours. Drain chicken and cook as desired. Makes about 1 cup for 1 small chicken.

POLYNESIAN MARINADE FOR CHICKEN

MARINADE

1/4 cup honey
1/4 cup fresh orange juice
2 tbs. fresh lemon juice
1/4 cup soy sauce
6 kumquats, finely chopped, or 2 tbs.
grated lemon peel
2 tbs. grated orange peel
1/2 tsp. ground ginger
1/4 tsp. pepper

1-2 chickens

Blend ingredients well in a blender. Marinate chicken in the refrigerator for a minimum of 2 hours. Drain chicken and cook as desired. Makes 1 1/2 cups for 1 to 2 chickens.

ITALIAN TARRAGON MARINADE FOR CHICKEN

MARINADE
½ cup olive oil
¼ cup vinegar, or dry vermouth or
white wine
1 tsp. dried tarragon
1 tsp. chopped fresh parsley
½ tsp. dried thyme
½ tsp. celery seeds

1 small chicken, or 2 chicken breasts

Mix ingredients together and marinate chicken in the refrigerator for a minimum of 2 hours. Drain chicken and cook as desired. Makes ¾ cup for 1 chicken.

NOTE: For a fat-free marinade, substitute chicken broth for olive oil.

FAT-FREE LEMON MARINADE FOR CHICKEN

MARINADE

¾ cup wine vinegar
3 tbs. lemon juice
1 medium onion, minced
1 clove garlic, crushed
¼ cup chopped fresh parsley
1 bay leaf
⅛ tsp. dried thyme
⅛ tsp. dried tarragon
2 tsp. salt
½ tsp. pepper

1 small chicken, or 2 chicken breasts

Mix marinade and pour over food. Let stand, covered, for at least 2 hours in the refrigerator. Drain chicken and cook as desired. Makes ¾ cup for 1 chicken.

NOTE: For even less fat, remove skin and any visible fat from chicken before marinating.

DRY MARINADE FOR CHICKEN

MARINADE
1 tbs. vegetable oil
2 tbs. brandy, lemon juice or lime
juice
1 clove garlic, crushed
1 tsp. salt
1/2 tsp. crushed cumin seed
1/2 tsp. dried tarragon, or basil

1 chicken

Pierce chicken skin with a fork or remove skin. Combine ingredients and brush on poultry. Cover and refrigerate overnight. Cook as desired. Makes enough for 1 chicken or 2 servings of chicken parts.

JAM-BOREE BAKED CHICKEN

MARINADE 1 - RED	MARINADE 2 - GREEN
1 bottle (8 oz.) prepared red salad dressing (such as Russian) ½ cup red or purple preserves, or jelly (strawberry, grape, plum, or a combination, or use ¼ cup jalapeño jelly) 1 envelope dry onion soup mix	1 bottle (8 oz.) prepared green salad dressing (such as Green Goddess) ½ cup light-colored preserves, or jam (apricot, pineapple, peach) 1 envelope dry onion soup mix

1-2 chickens, cut into pieces

Mix marinade ingredients in a small bowl. Lay chicken pieces in a flat pan in a single layer and spread with marinade. Cover and refrigerate for 3 hours. Bake with marinade at 350° for 45 minutes to 1 hour. Makes 4 to 6 servings.

ORIENTAL SPICED CHICKEN

MARINADE

1 cup light soy sauce
1 cup dry white wine, or sherry
2 cloves garlic, minced
2 tsp. minced ginger root

3-4 whole chicken breasts, split and boned, or 6-8 chicken legs with thighs attached

SAUCE

1 cup dry white wine, or dry sherry
½ cup hoisin sauce
½ cup ketchup

¼ cup dark brown sugar, firmly packed
1 clove garlic, minced

Mix marinade and pour over chicken. Refrigerate, covered, for at least 4 hours or overnight, turning chicken occasionally. Drain marinade and discard. Arrange chicken, skin side down, in a baking dish. Combine sauce ingredients and pour ½ over chicken. Bake at 350° for 25 minutes and turn chicken skin side up. Add remaining sauce and bake for another 25 minutes or until tender, basting occasionally. Serve with sauce. Makes 6 to 8 servings.

BAKED HONEY CHICKEN

MARINADE

¼ cup soy sauce
½ cup ketchup
¼ cup fresh lemon juice
¼ cup honey, or brown sugar

2 frying chickens, halved or cut into pieces
cold water
1 tbs. cornstarch
hot cooked rice

Pour marinade over chicken, which has been arranged in a single layer in a flat dish. Refrigerate several hours or overnight. Cover with foil and bake for 1 hour at 325°. Remove foil, baste with sauce and bake uncovered for 10 to 15 minutes or until tender and browned. To thicken sauce, mix a little cold water with 1 tbs. cornstarch and stir into sauce. Serve over hot cooked rice. Makes 4 to 6 servings.

BAKED TERIYAKI-WHISKEY CHICKEN

MARINADE
⅔ cup vegetable oil
⅔ cup soy sauce
⅔ cup bourbon
1 tsp. minced garlic
½ tsp. pepper

1 large frying chicken

Cut chicken into serving pieces, place in a single layer in a pan, and pour marinade mixture over each piece. Refrigerate for 4 hours or overnight. Bake in marinade, covered, in a 350° oven for 45 minutes or until chicken is well done. Turn pieces frequently and baste with sauce. Uncover and continue baking until brown, about 10 minutes. Makes 4 servings.

CALIFORNIA BARBECUED CHICKEN

MARINADE

½ cup sherry
⅓ cup honey
2 tbs. lime juice
2 tsp. cinnamon
½ tsp. curry powder
½ tsp. minced garlic

2-3 lb. frying chicken, cut into pieces or quartered

Combine marinade ingredients and pour over chicken. Cover and refrigerate for 4 hours. Broil or grill 6 inches from heat until tender. Baste often with remaining marinade. Chicken will brown quickly, so watch it closely. Makes 4 servings.

TANDOORI CHICKEN BREASTS

MARINADE
1 cup plain yogurt
juice of 1 lime
2 green chile peppers, chopped
2 cloves garlic, minced
1 tsp. minced ginger root
1½ tsp. ground coriander

4 chicken breasts, quartered
¼ cup margarine, melted

Skin chicken breasts and slash chicken diagonally with shallow cuts. Blend ½ of the yogurt with remaining ingredients. When well blended, add to remaining yogurt and stir to blend. Brush onto cut side of chicken and marinate for 8 hours or overnight. Remove chicken from marinade and broil or grill for 30 to 40 minutes. Coat with melted margarine before cooking. Brush with marinade while cooking and turn once. Makes 6 to 8 servings.

FRENCH NUTTY CHICKEN SALAD

MARINADE

2 tbs. wine vinegar
4 tbs. olive oil
1 tbs. fresh lemon juice

1 clove garlic, mashed
½ tsp. salt
½ tsp. pepper

meat from 2 cooked chickens, cubed
2 cups chopped celery
½ cup chopped green bell pepper
1 tbs. grated onion
4 large pimiento-stuffed olives, sliced
1 tsp. salt
½ tsp. pepper
1 grapefruit, pared and sectioned
1 tbs. Worcestershire sauce

dash hot pepper sauce
1 cup chopped pecans or almonds
4 hard-cooked eggs, chopped
seedless green grapes, halved, optional
½ cup low calorie mayonnaise
½-¾ cup nonfat plain yogurt or sour cream
paprika, olives, avocado slices, tomato wedges or fresh parsley for garnish

Prepare marinade and marinate chicken for several hours. Drain. Add celery, green pepper, onion, olives, salt, pepper and grapefruit. Stir gently to combine. Add Worcestershire, hot pepper sauce, nuts, eggs, grapes, mayonnaise and yogurt. Mix gently. Garnish with paprika, olives, avocado slices, eggs, tomato wedges or parsley. Makes 12 servings.

BANGKOK CURRIED CHICKEN AND FRUIT SALAD

MARINADE

½ cup mayonnaise
1 tbs. lime or lemon juice
2 tbs. curry powder
salt to taste

2 cups diced cooked chicken
1 cup shredded coconut
1 cup blanched golden raisins
1 cup chopped peanuts

1 cup sliced bananas
1 cup diced apples
1 cup diced celery
1 cup chutney

Mix marinade and add to all other ingredients. Toss lightly and marinate in the refrigerator overnight. Makes 12 to 15 servings.

NOTE: This recipe may be doubled for an elegant addition to a buffet supper for a crowd.

GRILLED TURKEY WINGS

MARINADE
¼ cup lime juice
1 clove garlic, crushed
¼ tsp. dried thyme
salt and pepper to taste
2 tbs. vegetable oil

6 turkey wings

Cut off wing tips and reserve for making stock. Cut apart remaining 2 joints of wings. Place wings in a shallow dish and add lime juice, garlic, thyme, salt and pepper. Toss to mix well. Cover and marinate for at least 30 minutes. Drain wing pieces and place on a greased grill. Brush with oil and grill until lightly browned. Turn and grill other side. Brush occasionally with marinade and/or more oil. Continue to grill until meat in the thickest portion of wing sections is tender, about 1 hour total cooking time. Makes 6 servings.

TERIYAKI TURKEY

MARINADE
1½ cups soy sauce
½ cup lemon juice
¼ tsp. ground ginger
2 cloves garlic, minced
¼ cup minced fresh parsley

1 turkey hindquarter

Place turkey hindquarter in a shallow dish. Mix marinade and pour over turkey. Turn to coat well. Cover and marinate in the refrigerator for several hours or overnight. Drain. Grill until tender and browned, 1½ to 2 hours. Turn and baste with marinade as necessary to prevent burning. When turkey feels tender when pressed, cut into the thigh joint. If no red juices run, turkey is done. Slice across thigh and lengthwise on drumstick to serve. Makes 3 to 4 servings.

FISH AND SHELLFISH ENTRÉES

Fish fillets and shellfish, especially flavorful when added to marinades, are easy to prepare in the oven or on the grill. White wines, lemon and lime juices and the same flavorings normally associated with fish are used in the marinades. The added liquids help prevent delicate fish from drying out during the cooking process.

Fresh fish fillets are preferable, though frozen fish that has been thawed and patted dry may be used. When you select fresh fish, keep in mind that it should not have a typical fishy smell, which suggests that the fish are not fresh. Fresh fish should be firm. If the head is on the fish when it is purchased, the eyes should be prominent rather than shrunken, and the area behind the gills should be very red.

GENERAL DIRECTIONS FOR MARINATING AND COOKING FISH

When you unwrap the fish at home, do not rinse it under running water; instead, fill a pan with a solution of 1 qt. water and 1 tbs. lemon juice and rinse the fish in that. Pat dry. Prepare the marinade and let the fish soak for only an hour or two, refrigerated and covered.

Fish is already tender and delicate, so it does not require the lengthy marinating times that meats and poultry need. If the marinade does not cover the fish, either turn the fish over once during the marinating time or baste the fish with the marinade.

The greatest danger in preparing fish is overcooking it. Uncooked fish is translucent; the second it becomes opaque, it is done. The only accurate way of testing is to flake the thickest part with a fork or toothpick to check the color and texture. If a recipe calls for 10 minutes of cooking time, check it at 5 minutes and watch it carefully.

Generally, fish experts suggest a ratio of 10 minutes baking, broiling or grilling time to each inch of thickness. Measure the thickest part of the fish. A whole salmon that measures 4 inches thick will cook for 40 minutes. A 1½-inch-thick halibut steak requires approximately 15 minutes total or 7½ minutes per side. Check it early.

PORTUGUESE LEMON MARINADE FOR FISH

MARINADE

6 tbs. vegetable oil, or olive oil
juice and grated rind of 1 lemon
3 tbs. vinegar
1/4 cup chopped fresh parsley
2 green onions, chopped
1 tsp. salt
1/2 tsp. crushed peppercorns, or
white pepper
1/8 tsp. dried thyme

whole fish, thick fish fillets, or fish steaks such as
albacore, greyfish, snapper, yellowtail and tuna

Combine ingredients and place over fish in a shallow dish. Cover and refrigerate for 2 to 4 hours. Drain and bake or broil fish according to directions on page 129. Makes 3/4 cup marinade.

TERIYAKI MARINADE FOR FISH

MARINADE
6 tbs. soy sauce
6 tbs. water, or white wine
2 cloves garlic, crushed
¼ cup fresh lime juice

whole fish, fish fillets, fish steaks or shellfish

Mix soy sauce, water or wine and garlic. Add fish or shellfish and marinate for 2 to 3 hours in the refrigerator. Drain and bake or broil fish according to directions on page 129. Use lime juice to baste fish while cooking. Makes ¾ cup marinade.

HAWAIIAN MARINADE FOR FISH

MARINADE
1 cup pineapple juice
¼ cup vegetable oil
1 envelope (1½ oz.) dry spaghetti
sauce mix, or ½ cup prepared
spaghetti sauce without meat

fish fillets

Combine ingredients and marinate fish fillets for 1 to 2 hours in the refrigerator. Drain marinade and use for basting. Bake or broil fish according to directions on page 129. Makes 1½ cups marinade.

BEER MARINADE FOR SHELLFISH

MARINADE

1/2 cup vegetable oil
2 cups beer
2 tbs. lemon juice
1 medium onion, thinly sliced
1 garlic clove, halved
1/2 tsp. salt
1/4 tsp. pepper

shelled and deveined shrimp, or other shellfish

Mix ingredients and pour over shellfish. Marinate in the refrigerator 2 to 3 hours. Drain. Grill, broil or sauté shellfish. Makes 2 cups.

FAT-FREE MARINADE FOR FISH

MARINADE
¾ cup instant chicken broth
6 tbs. lemon juice
1 tbs. fennel seeds or celery seeds
½ tsp. ground coriander, or dried tarragon
salt and pepper to taste

about 1 lb. fish

Mix all ingredients and pour over fish. Refrigerate, covered, for 1 to 2 hours. Turn occasionally. Drain and cook according to directions on page 129. Makes ¾ cup marinade for about 1 lb. fish.

BROILED HALIBUT STEAKS WITH SAKE

MARINADE
6 tbs. olive oil
6 tbs. sake, or dry white wine
2 tbs. lime or lemon juice
2 small garlic cloves, finely chopped
1 tsp. dried basil
1 tsp. freshly ground pepper
1½ tsp. salt

2 halibut steaks, 1 inch thick
oil or butter

Combine marinade ingredients and place fish in a single layer in a flat glass dish. Pour marinade over steaks and marinate for 2 hours, turning 2 or 3 times. Line a broiler pan or rack with foil; oil or butter foil. Remove steaks from marinade and place on foil. Broil 4 inches from heat, about 5 minutes on each side or until done, brushing with marinade during cooking. Makes 4 servings.

NOTE: This procedure may be used for preparing any fish steaks.

SESAME MARINADE FOR FISH FILLETS

MARINADE

¼ cup vegetable oil
⅓ cup lemon juice
1 tbs. grated lemon peel
1 tbs. soy sauce
4 tsp. sugar
2 tbs. toasted sesame seeds
2 tbs. chopped fresh parsley
½ tsp. salt

1½ lb. fish fillets in slices or large pieces for broiling, or
1-inch cubes for skewering

Mix marinade ingredients and pour over fish. Marinate for 1 hour. Remove from marinade and broil or grill. Makes 3 to 4 servings.

FRIED SCALLOPS

MARINADE
1/4 cup olive oil
1/4 cup dry sherry
2 tbs. lemon juice

1 lb. scallops
salt, celery salt and pepper to taste
2 eggs, beaten, or egg whites only

breadcrumbs
vegetable oil for deep fat frying

DRESSING

1/4 cup chili sauce
3/4 cup mayonnaise

2 tsp. red wine vinegar

If scallops are large, cut each into 3 or 4 pieces. Wash scallops well and drain on paper towels. Mix marinade and let scallops soak for 1/2 hour. Drain well. Sprinkle with salt, celery salt and pepper. Dip scallops into beaten eggs, and then into breadcrumbs, coating thoroughly. Chill until ready to serve. For dressing, stir chili sauce into mayonnaise until well blended; stir in vinegar. Chill. Heat oil to 370°. Fry scallops until medium brown. Pass dressing separately. Makes 4 to 6 servings.

TUNA FISH-PINEAPPLE TOSS

MARINADE

¼ cup vegetable oil
3 tbs. tarragon vinegar
3 tbs. juice from canned pineapple
½ tsp. ground cloves
1 tbs. crème de menthe, or fresh
mint leaves, or 1 tsp. mint extract

1 can (13½ oz.) water-packed tuna fish
1 can (4-oz.) pineapple chunks in natural syrup, drained, syrup reserved
lettuce
fresh mint leaves, tomatoes, and other vegetables as desired for garnish

Drain tuna fish. Mix marinade and pour over tuna; stir. Cover and refrigerate for 4 to 6 hours. Remove from marinade with a slotted spoon. Drain pineapple chunks and gently mix into tuna. Serve on a bed of lettuce garnished with mint leaves, tomatoes and other vegetables in season. Makes 2 to 3 servings.

BARBECUED GARLIC SHRIMP

MARINADE

1 cup white wine
1 tbs. chili sauce
1 lime or lemon, sliced
2 cloves garlic, minced
½ tsp. salt
½ tsp. pepper
½ tsp. paprika
dash dried oregano

1 lb. large raw shrimp

Prepare shrimp: Cut heads off with a very sharp knife; slice down the back and remove black vein by rinsing shrimp under cold running water. Leave shells and tails on. Mix marinade ingredients and marinate shrimp for 1 hour or more. Remove from marinade and broil or grill, turning and basting often. Or, bake in a 300° oven for about 30 minutes, basting often. Makes 4 servings.

BOSTON-STYLE MARINATED MUSSELS

MARINADE

¼ cup vegetable oil, or olive oil
1 tbs. dry vermouth
3 tbs. snipped fresh chives

1 tbs. snipped fresh parsley
¼ tsp. salt
¼ tsp. white pepper

2 cups dry white wine
½ cup minced green onions
8 sprigs fresh parsley
1 bay leaf
¼ tsp. dried thyme

⅛ tsp. white peppercorns
4 qt. scrubbed mussels, soaked in 3 or
  4 changes of cold water
2 tbs. lemon juice
lettuce

Bring wine, green onions, parsley, bay leaf, thyme and peppercorns to a boil in a large pot over high heat. Add mussels, bring to a boil, cover and steam for 2 minutes. Uncover and stir until shells open, about 5 minutes. Discard unopened mussels. Shell mussels; transfer to a large bowl and discard shells. Strain cooking liquid through coffee filters or cheesecloth into a large enamel or stainless steel saucepan; add lemon juice. Cook sauce over medium heat until reduced to 1 cup, about 20 minutes. Add marinade and pour over mussels. Refrigerate, covered, stirring occasionally, for about 2 hours or until cold. Transfer to a lettuce-lined bowl. Makes 4 to 6 servings.

NORTHWEST FISH STEAK GRILL

MARINADE

1 cup dry vermouth
¾ cup vegetable oil
⅓ cup lemon juice
2 tbs. chopped chives
2 tsp. salt
1 clove garlic, finely chopped

¼ tsp. dried marjoram
¼ tsp. pepper
¼ tsp. dried thyme
⅛ tsp. dried sage
⅛ tsp. hot pepper sauce

2 lb. salmon, halibut, or other fish steaks, fresh or frozen

Thaw steaks if frozen. Cut into serving-sized portions and place in a single layer in a shallow baking dish. Combine marinade ingredients and pour over fish. Refrigerate, covered, for 4 hours, turning occasionally. Remove fish and reserve sauce for basting. Place fish on a well-greased hinged wire grill. Cook about 4 inches from moderately hot coals for 8 minutes. Baste with sauce. Turn and cook for 7 to 10 minutes longer, or until fish flakes easily when tested with a fork. Makes 6 servings.

SWORDFISH WITH TOMATO SAUCE

MARINADE

¼ cup vegetable oil
2 tbs. lemon juice
2 tsp. Worcestershire sauce
¼ cup minced onion
2 cloves garlic, crushed
2 tsp. sugar
¼ tsp. pepper

2 lb. swordfish (greyfish)

Mix marinade and pour over fish. Marinate for 1 hour in the refrigerator, turning occasionally. Drain fish, reserving marinade for basting. Broil or grill fish 5 inches from heat for 15 to 20 minutes on each side or until it flakes easily with a fork. Makes 6 servings.

KABOBS

GENERAL DIRECTIONS FOR KABOBS

Almost anything that can be skewered and cooked is a kabob candidate, including meat, poultry, fish, vegetables and fruits. Treatment of meat and poultry is essentially the same for all kabobs: the meat is cut into chunks about 1 to 2 inches square and marinated for several hours (for about 2 hours if poultry) or overnight in the refrigerator. The meat is threaded onto the presoaked wooden skewer or metal skewer with or without vegetables and fruits, and then grilled or broiled. The kabob must be turned once or twice while broiling so all sides are cooked. Because many vegetables cook more quickly than meats, they must be watched carefully and brushed with the marinade frequently during cooking. Vegetables and fruits can be cooked on separate skewers and served with the cooked meat cubes.

The marinades for red meat can be interchanged with any of various cuts of meat. Generally 2 cups of liquid marinade will cover about 1 pound of meat cubes. Remember that marinades tenderize, so you can select less costly cuts of beef. Trim away excess fat and bones, cut into cubes, soak in marinade and skewer.

Some additional kabob tips:

- Presoak wooden skewers to prevent burning.
- Prevent ingredients from slipping off skewers by placing a large cube of bread brushed with oil at the pointed end.

- Frozen fish tends to become softer than fresh fish and is more likely to slip off the skewers. To secure fish pieces, thread them alternately with firm foods such as chunks of zucchini, green bell pepper, pineapple, etc.
- Vegetables that require longer cooking than others, such as onions, potatoes and zucchini, should be parboiled or placed on separate skewers. Begin to cook them before cooking the meat or chicken.
- Always preheat the broiler; oil the pan or grill to prevent meat from sticking.
- Keep slippery foods, such as raw oysters or chicken livers, under control by wrapping them in bacon or other meat. Intersperse soft foods, such as fish, with harder foods, such as zucchini, to give them all a firmer hold.
- Select ingredients for color and texture; combine crunchy things with soft, smooth foods. Complement flavors: sweet and sour, smoky and nutty, zesty and mild.
- Combine fruits and vegetables with meats, chicken and fish.
- Serve your kabobs with white, brown or wild rice, African couscous or felafel.
- Baste the foods with marinade during cooking to keep them moist.

ONION SOUP KABOB MARINADE

MARINADE

1 envelope dry onion soup mix

1 cup vegetable oil

½ cup red wine vinegar

1 tbs. soy sauce

MUSTARD KABOB MARINADE

MARINADE

¼ cup ketchup

¼ cup vinegar

¼ cup vegetable oil

¼ cup water

1 tbs. prepared mustard

1½ tsp. salt

for each recipe:

1-1½ lb. beef, cut into 1- or 2-inch cubes

Mix ingredients and marinate beef cubes in the refrigerator for several hours or overnight. Drain and cook according to directions on page 144. Makes 3 to 4 servings.

PEPPERY YOGURT KABOB MARINADE

MARINADE
1½ cups plain yogurt
¾ cup chopped onion
1 tsp. minced garlic
½ dried hot chile pepper, chopped
¾ tsp. cumin seed
½ tsp. nutmeg
¼ tsp. salt
¼ tsp. cinnamon

1-1½ lb. beef, cut into 1- or 2-inch cubes

Mix ingredients and marinate beef cubes in the refrigerator for several hours or overnight. Drain and cook according to directions on page 144. Makes 3 to 4 servings.

SPICED KABOB MARINADE

MARINADE

1/3 cup soy sauce
1/4 cup lemon juice
1 tbs. brown sugar
2 tsp. minced garlic
2 tsp. ground caraway seeds
2 tsp. ground coriander seeds
1/2 tsp. salt
1/4 tsp. dried red pepper flakes

1-1½ lb. beef, cut into 1- or 2-inch cubes

Mix ingredients and marinate beef cubes in the refrigerator for several hours or overnight. Drain and cook according to directions on page 144. Makes 3 to 4 servings.

INDONESIAN SATÉ LAMB KABOBS

MARINADE

½ cup soy sauce mixed with 1 tsp.
  dark molasses
¾ cup hot water
½ cup chopped or ground peanuts
  without skins, toasted in oven

⅓ cup chunky-style peanut butter
1 tsp. dried red pepper flakes
1 garlic clove, minced
2 tbs. lemon juice

1½ lb. lamb shoulder or leg, cut into 1-inch cubes
½ cup tomato sauce
¼ cup beef stock or water
1 tsp. hot pepper sauce

Combine marinade ingredients in a saucepan. Bring to a boil and stir until fairly smooth. Allow to cool. Pour ½ of the mixture over lamb cubes and marinate at least 2 hours. Add tomato sauce, stock or water and hot pepper sauce to marinade in saucepan. Remove lamb cubes from marinade and add that marinade to saucepan. Boil for 3 minutes, stirring. Use for basting and as a dipping sauce when serving. Place marinated cubes on small presoaked wooden skewers and broil. Makes 4 to 6 servings.

LAMB KABOBS WITH BEER-PINEAPPLE MARINADE

MARINADE
½ cup beer
½ cup juice from fresh pineapple
2 tbs. vegetable oil
1 tbs. soy sauce
1 clove garlic, crushed

1½ lb. lamb shoulder or leg, cut into 1½-inch cubes
1 large green bell pepper
2 large tomatoes
2 small onions
8 cubes fresh pineapple, 2 inches each

Mix marinade ingredients. Add lamb and refrigerate, covered, overnight. Seed and cut pepper into 2-inch cubes. Quarter tomatoes. Peel and quarter onions. Drain marinade and reserve. Alternate lamb, vegetables and pineapple pieces on skewers. Brush with marinade while broiling. Makes 4 servings.

LAMB-HAM KABOBS

MARINADE

reserved pineapple syrup from
  pineapple chunks
1 can (10½ oz.) mushroom gravy
1 tbs. soy sauce

1 tsp. curry powder
1 clove garlic, minced
dash ground ginger

1 lb. lamb shoulder or leg, cut into 1½-inch cubes
½ lb. cooked ham, cut into 1-inch cubes
1 small apple, cut into 8 wedges
1 can (8 oz.) pineapple chunks in heavy syrup, drained, syrup reserved

Drain pineapple and combine juice with other marinade ingredients. Add lamb and ham. Marinate for 6 hours or overnight, covered, in the refrigerator. Drain. Arrange ham and lamb alternately on 2 skewers. On separate skewers, arrange pineapple chunks and apple slices. Broil meat skewers over coals or in oven for 5 minutes, turning and brushing with marinade. Place fruit kabobs over heat and cook meat and fruit 10 minutes more or until lamb is done. Makes 4 servings.

APPLE-FLAVORED CHICKEN KABOBS

MARINADE

¼ cup vegetable oil
1 cup dry red wine
2 tbs. vinegar
2 tbs. soy sauce

1 can (6 oz.) frozen apple juice
  concentrate, thawed
dash ground ginger

4 whole chicken breasts, halved,
  skinned
salt and pepper to taste
8 mushrooms

8 small white onions
8 cherry tomatoes
2 oranges, peeled and quartered
2 pineapple slices, quartered

Bone chicken breasts and cut each half-breast into 4 pieces. Sprinkle chicken with salt and pepper. Alternate chicken pieces with mushrooms, onions, cherry tomatoes, orange quarters and pineapple quarters to make 8 skewers. Place skewers in a shallow pan. Combine marinade ingredients and spoon over kabobs. Let stand for 1 hour. Drain and broil or grill 6 inches from heat for 15 minutes on each side. Brush with marinade every 5 minutes. Makes 8 servings.

PERSIAN CHICKEN KABOBS

MARINADE

¼ cup vegetable oil
¼ cup tarragon wine vinegar
½ tsp. dried mint leaves

¼ tsp. dried rosemary
1 clove garlic, crushed
¼ tsp. hot pepper sauce

4 chicken breasts, halved, skinned and boned, cut into 2-inch pieces
1 tsp. salt
4 medium tomatoes, quartered
16 small white onions, peeled

6 green bell peppers, seeded and cut into skewer pieces
16 small to medium mushroom caps
rice pilaf, or plain cooked rice

Sprinkle chicken with ½ tsp. salt. Mix marinade and pour over chicken in a flat dish. Refrigerate for at least 2 hours or overnight, turning once or twice. Drain and reserve liquid for basting.

Thread chicken pieces on skewers, alternating with tomatoes, onions, green peppers and mushroom caps. Brush with marinade. Sprinkle with remaining ½ tsp. salt. Broil or grill about 6 inches from heat for 30 minutes or until chicken is done, turning and basting while cooking. Serve with rice pilaf or cooked rice.

DILLED SHRIMP KABOBS

MARINADE

1 cup olive oil, or vegetable oil
1/4 cup cider vinegar
2 tbs. lemon juice
1/2 cup snipped fresh dill

2 cloves garlic, crushed
2 tsp. Dijon-style mustard
1 tbs. snipped fresh parsley

12 jumbo shrimp (about 2 lb.)
6 small lemons
2 large green bell peppers, seeded and
cut into 1-inch squares

12 mushrooms, halved
snipped fresh dill for garnish
cooked rice

Cut heads off shrimp with a very sharp knife; slice down the back and remove black vein by rinsing shrimp under cold running water. Leave shell and tail on. Mix marinade, pour over shrimp in a bowl and marinate overnight in the refrigerator. Drain. Cut a thin slice off one end of each lemon and thread 1 lemon lengthwise onto each of 6 skewers. Alternate pieces of bell pepper, mushrooms and shrimp on each skewer with bell pepper piece at end to anchor shrimp. Grill for 5 to 6 minutes with shrimp tails up. Turn skewers and test shrimp with a sharp knife at center back until shrimp flesh looks opaque. Garnish with snipped dill. Serve with rice. Makes 6 servings.

MARINATED FRUITS AND FRUIT DESSERTS

Fresh fruits marinated in the juices of other fruits or in brandies and liqueurs are tantalizing taste treats at the end of any meal. They are also between-meal tempters. Some purists argue that the fruit itself is delicious enough without any additions, but soaking fruits in zesty marinades is favored by an overwhelming majority of dessert connoisseurs.

The possible combinations are infinite. You can be as creative as you dare in the dishes you prepare, because almost any fruit can be combined with any other and all can be combined in the marinades. Marinated fruits may be eaten as they come from the refrigerator and steeping liquid. They can be placed on skewers and grilled as a kabob or fried as fritters (beignets).

Once you have tasted these delectable desserts, you can wed the fruits and their liquids with cakes and puddings, or spoon the mashed fruits that have been soaked in the liquids over cobblers and ice creams.

The words steeping or macerating, rather than marinating, are found in many cookbooks. Regardless of the term, the procedure is the same and the results are incredible.

Liqueurs, a fruit marinade themselves, make a delicious marinade for other fruits.

BASIC FRUIT JUICE MARINADE

MARINADE

½ cup orange juice, or other fruit
juice
grated rind and juice of ½ lemon
¼ cup maple or corn syrup
1 vanilla bean, or 6 coriander seeds,
crushed
¼ cup brandy or liqueur, optional

fresh fruit, peeled and sliced, diced or quartered

Thoroughly mix all ingredients and pour juice over fruit. Marinate in the refrigerator, covered, for 4 hours, occasionally stirring gently. Let stand at room temperature for about 20 minutes before serving.

MARINATED STRAWBERRIES

MARINADE
1½ oz. vodka
1½ oz. Triple Sec, or other orange-
flavored liqueur
1½ oz. rum

4 cups whole fresh strawberries
½ cup confectioners' sugar
whipped cream

Wash and hull strawberries and toss with sugar. Mix spirits and pour over strawberries in a bowl. Chill for at least 1 hour. Serve with whipped cream. Makes 6 to 8 servings.

MACEDOINE OF FRESH FRUITS

> **MARINADE**
> 2 tbs. wine, or any flavor liqueur

1½ cups fresh fruit in season

Fruit marinated in wine or liqueur can be created in an infinite variety of combinations. The fruit should be top-of-the-season, ripe, perfect, pared and seeded. Favorites are strawberries, raspberries, plums, seedless green grapes, peaches, apricots, avocado slices, orange and grapefruit sections, melon balls, cherries and nectarines. Prick fruits to allow the wine or liqueur to soak in for at least 1 hour. Raw apples and pears require longer marinating periods than softer fruits. A macedoine is usually served cold, but you may flambé it if the fruit is at room temperature. Makes 4 servings.

SUGGESTED COMBINATIONS

- oranges marinated in cognac
- cherries marinated in brandy
- peaches studded with cloves, marinated in mint-flavored liqueur
- melon balls marinated in port wine

SPICED ORANGE SLICES

MARINADE
½ cup sugar
1 cup Burgundy wine, or claret
1 vanilla bean
1 stick cinnamon
12 whole cloves
1 lemon, thinly sliced

6 oranges, peeled and sliced about ¼-inch thick
½ cup raisins, optional
whipped cream

In a saucepan, mix marinade ingredients together, bring to a boil and simmer for 15 minutes. Remove lemon and spices and pour sauce over orange slices and raisins. Marinate, refrigerated, for 24 hours. Baste occasionally. Serve with whipped cream. Makes 4 to 6 servings.

HONEY AND WINE BERRY MARINADE

MARINADE

½ cup orange honey
½ cup sweet sherry, or orange juice

2 cups berries (strawberries, raspberries, blueberries or other)

Combine honey with sherry. Pour over prepared fruit and marinate in the refrigerator for at least 1 hour. Serve chilled. Makes 4 servings.

MARINATED FRUIT WITH
WHIPPED CREAM CUSTARD

MARINADE

¼ cup fruit-flavored liqueur (kirsch,
orange, peach, etc.)
2 tbs. sugar

2 cups fresh fruit in season (pineapple, pears, peaches,
plums, or a mixture), cut into cubes

Sprinkle fruit with liqueur and sugar and marinate for 4 hours, covered, in the refrigerator. Stir gently often so marinade permeates fruit.

WHIPPED CREAM CUSTARD

2 cups sifted confectioners' sugar
1 cup milk
6 tbs. butter or margarine
4 egg yolks, beaten
2 tsp. vanilla extract
1 tsp. fruit-flavored liqueur
1/2 cup heavy cream, whipped

Combine sugar and milk in a saucepan over medium heat. Add butter and stir until melted. Stir 2 tbs. hot mixture into egg yolks. Add yolks to hot milk mixture, stirring until mixture thickens. Cool and refrigerate for 3 to 4 hours. Just before serving, stir vanilla into custard and add liqueur to taste. Fold into whipped cream.

To serve: Place fruits in individual dessert dishes and spoon whipped cream custard on top. Makes 4 to 5 servings.

FRUIT UPSIDE-DOWN CAKE

MARINADE

¼ cup fruit-flavored liqueur (orange,
apricot or peach)

½ cup butter
1 cup light brown sugar, firmly packed
1 can (16 oz.) sliced pineapple, or peaches, or plums, drained
8 maraschino cherries, drained

BATTER

2 egg yolks
1 tsp. lemon juice
1 cup sugar
6 tbs. hot water
1 cup sifted flour
1½ tsp. baking powder
¼ tsp. salt
3 egg whites, beaten until stiff peaks form

Melt butter in a 9-inch-square pan and spread brown sugar over it. Cover with fruit and arrange cherries between fruit pieces. Dribble liqueur over fruit and let stand at room temperature for 1 hour. Preheat oven to 325°.

Beat egg yolks with lemon juice until thick and lemon-colored. Add sugar gradually; slowly stir in hot water. Beat until well mixed. Sift flour with baking powder and salt. Add to mixture and mix until batter is smooth. Fold in beaten egg whites. Pour batter over fruit. Bake for 45 minutes or until toothpick inserted in center comes out clean. Cool for 5 minutes. Turn out onto a platter so fruit is on top. Serve slightly warm. If desired, a topping made of whipped cream with 1 to 2 tbs. liqueur whipped in may be served. Makes 6 to 8 servings.

NOTE: Any fruit can be used for an upside-down cake, such as canned sliced pineapple, plums or peaches. Fruit can be marinated in a liqueur ahead of time. Some of the liqueur can be used in the cake batter.

Packaged cake mix may be used. Substitute ¼ cup liqueur along with the liquid called for in mix.

SWEET DESSERT FRITTERS

MARINADE
3/4 cup orange-flavored liqueur

1 lb. fresh fruit (apricots, plums, peaches, pears, apples)
3 tbs. sugar

BATTER

1 cup flour	1 egg yolk	vegetable oil for frying
1/2 tsp. salt	3/4 cup milk	1/3 cup confectioners'
1 1/2 tsp. sugar	1 egg white	sugar for glaze

Clean fruit; remove pits and seeds and cut pears, peaches and apple into bite-sized pieces. Cut apricots and plums in half. Skins may be left on. Put in a bowl and sprinkle with sugar and then with liqueur. Marinate in the refrigerator for 1 hour.

For batter: Mix flour, salt, sugar, egg yolk and milk thoroughly. Let stand for 1 hour. Add egg white, beaten lightly, to batter. Drain fruit and dip pieces into batter. Deep fry a few pieces at a time in vegetable oil at 375° until golden brown. Drain on paper towels. Arrange on a baking tray. Sprinkle with sugar and glaze either in a very hot oven or under a broiler. Makes 8 to 10 servings.

INDEX

SERVE CREATIVE, EASY, NUTRITIOUS MEALS WITH NITTY GRITTY® COOKBOOKS

Extra-Special Crockery Pot Recipes
Cooking in Clay
Marinades
Deep Fried Indulgences
Cooking with Parchment Paper
The Garlic Cookbook
Flatbreads From Around the World
From Your Ice Cream Maker
Favorite Cookie Recipes
Cappuccino/Espresso: The Book of Beverages
Indoor Grilling
Slow Cooking
The Best Pizza is Made at Home
The Well Dressed Potato
Convection Oven Cookery
The Steamer Cookbook
The Pasta Machine Cookbook
The Versatile Rice Cooker

The Dehydrator Cookbook
The Bread Machine Cookbook
The Bread Machine Cookbook II
The Bread Machine Cookbook III
The Bread Machine Cookbook IV
The Bread Machine Cookbook V
Worldwide Sourdoughs From Your Bread Machine
Recipes for the Pressure Cooker
The New Blender Book
The Sandwich Maker Cookbook
Waffles
The Coffee Book
The Juicer Book
The Juicer Book II
Bread Baking (traditional), revised
No Salt, No Sugar, No Fat Cookbook

Cooking for 1 or 2
Quick and Easy Pasta Recipes
The 9x13 Pan Cookbook
Chocolate Cherry Tortes and Other Lowfat Delights
Low Fat American Favorites
Now That's Italian!
Fabulous Fiber Cookery
Low Salt, Low Sugar, Low Fat Desserts
Healthy Cooking on the Run
Healthy Snacks for Kids
Muffins, Nut Breads and More
The Wok
New Ways to Enjoy Chicken
Favorite Seafood Recipes
New International Fondue Cookbook

Write or call for our free catalog.
BRISTOL PUBLISHING ENTERPRISES, INC.
P.O. Box 1737, San Leandro, CA 94577
(800) 346-4889; in California (510) 895-4461